Quilt Club

Scrappy Patterns Perfect for Block Swaps with Friends

Paula Barnes and Mary Ellen Robison
of *Red Crinoline Quilts*

Martingale®
Create with Confidence

Quilt Club: Scrappy Patterns Perfect for Block Swaps
with Friends
© 2021 by Paula Barnes and Mary Ellen Robison

Martingale®
18939 120th Ave. NE, Ste. 101
Bothell, WA 98011-9511 USA
ShopMartingale.com

Printed in Hong Kong
26 25 24 23 22 21   8 7 6 5 4 3 2 1

Library of Congress Cataloging-in-Publication Data
is available upon request.

ISBN: 978-1-68356-162-0

MISSION STATEMENT

We empower makers who use fabric and yarn
to make life more enjoyable.

CREDITS

**PUBLISHER AND
CHIEF VISIONARY OFFICER**
Jennifer Erbe Keltner

CONTENT DIRECTOR
Karen Costello Soltys

DESIGN MANAGER
Adrienne Smitke

TECHNICAL EDITOR
Nancy Mahoney

PRODUCTION MANAGER
Regina Girard

COPY EDITOR
Melissa Bryan

**COVER AND
BOOK DESIGNER**
Mia Mar

ILLUSTRATOR
Sandy Loi

PHOTOGRAPHERS
Brent Kane
Adam Albright

SPECIAL THANKS

*Photography for this book was taken at
the FarmHouse Cottage in Snohomish, Washington,
and the Garden Barn in Indianola, Iowa.*

Contents

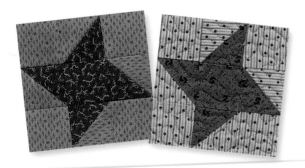

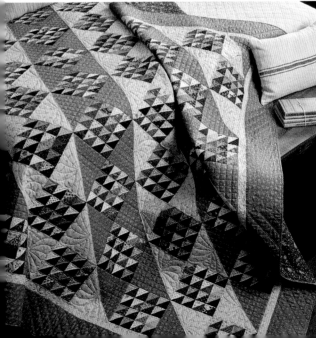

Introduction

Inspiration comes from many sources. When we decided that we wanted to write a third book and we wanted it to be different from the first two, we looked to the quilt community for our inspiration. For years we've traveled and attended quilt shows and numerous retreats. We've taught and shared our quilts all across the United States, and we've been members of many quilt guilds and quilt bees. What did all of these experiences have in common? Quilters—people who have become our friends. People who share a common interest, a passion for fabric and design and quilting, and the wish to share it with their friends.

We've all shared that passion in so many ways. We share our quilts at guild meetings and on Facebook and Instagram. We comment on what other people share and we join exchanges with those friends we've made through this process. So with all that in mind, *Quilt Club*, a book devoted to block and quilt exchanges, was born. We've all been participants in numerous exchanges and we've seen the good, the bad, and the ugly; now we only want the good. We want our exchanges to be successful, and we want yours to be successful too.

We looked back on past exchanges and talked to friends about successful exchanges they had participated in. We received a lot of feedback, and hopefully the information you'll discover in this book is the best process for a successful exchange. We've included everything from blocks that are perfect for beginning quilters to blocks that are definitely more challenging. You'll find big quilts (because everyone loves a big quilt but sometimes it's daunting to make one on your own, plus it's easier to get a good variety of fabrics for a big quilt when you share blocks with others) and smaller quilts that are perfect as table toppers and wall hangings. We even included exchanges that will work for a small group of participants or a larger group. You'll also discover tips for organizing your exchange, pointers for ensuring that your blocks will be nearly perfect, and some basic guidelines for a good exchange.

We love exchanges and can honestly say they have provided us with some of our most beautiful quilts. There's nothing better than looking at a quilt and knowing that it was created with friends. So, gather your friends, find a block that seems to call your name, and start your next exchange. Share your finished projects with the quilting community!

~ *Paula and Mary Ellen*

How to Do an Exchange

So, we've sparked your interest and you want to be part of an exchange group, but you're wondering where to begin. Many of our first exchanges were with a quilt bee that we belonged to. We usually began with one of the members finding a block or quilt they were interested in making and then presenting it to the group. Interested members would sign up, form a group, and the exchange would begin. Many groups will have members take turns presenting a new exchange for the group to participate in. We've participated in birthday exchanges, holiday exchanges, and so on.

Once you have a group, we recommend you choose a leader and it most likely should be the person that suggested the block or quilt. The group will talk and decide on key elements (how many blocks, how many participants, when it's due, what kind of fabrics and colors will be used, etc.), and it will be up to the leader to provide all of the information in written form to the whole group. We created a worksheet that you can download and print for all the participants (go to ShopMartingale.com/QuiltClub). Make sure that *each* participant has their own copy of this book so they'll have access to the pattern you're making.

On page 7, you'll find the guidelines we like to use, which everyone in the group can read and agree to before the exchange begins. Deciding on fabrics, colors, starching or not starching, etc., are all easy choices, but it's important to include guidelines with your exchange information. We cannot stress enough the importance of being kind to each other. We all have different skill levels, and we need to remember that when joining an exchange. If you know that you cannot handle anything but perfect blocks, then

perhaps you shouldn't participate. Remember to do your best piecing and assume that everyone else is doing the same. When all is said and done, your quilt will be beautiful.

After you've finished your blocks, by the due date of course, it's time to get organized for the exchange. You will need a reclosable bag for every participant, including yourself–so 10 participants means you'll need 10 bags. Write the name of each participant on a separate bag along with your name. For example, "To Mary Ellen from Paula." Your bag will include your set also, and it will say, "To Paula from Paula." (After years of organizing exchanges, please trust us when we say this step is necessary. It will make the distribution easier when you have everyone's block sets.) Once you've labeled your bags, place one block from each set you made in each bag. Follow the directions that were provided to you at the beginning of the exchange. Bring all of your bags the day of the exchange and give them to the leader. We recommend that the leader and one assistant distribute the bags. If everyone has followed the directions, you should go home with all the blocks you need to complete the quilt.

Another exchange option is a fabric exchange. The group can pick a theme, a fabric collection, or a color scheme, and then decide on the fabric size (anything from fat quarters to strips), the number of participants, and the number of fabrics that each participant will bring.

A follow-up meeting in a year would be a great time to have a show-and-tell with the quilts the group made from the exchange. We wish you the best of luck with your exchange.

Block Exchange Guidelines

We love participating in block exchanges, but it's important to set some rules so that everyone knows what's expected of them. That way, everyone can expect to receive quality blocks from all the participants. We've put together this list of guidelines to make your block exchanges go smoothly.

- Use only quilt-shop quality, 100% cotton fabric, unless other fabric is requested.

- Decide as a group whether you'll be starching fabrics; we highly recommend starching before cutting or piecing, as it aids in accurate sewing.

- For a quilt with half-square-triangle units, decide whether you'll be using the traditional method or prefer using triangle papers, such as Star Singles.

- As a group, decide what type of fabric to use in your exchange—reproduction, batiks, seasonal, novelty, etc. Be sure to specify any fabrics that should not be used.

- Use your best fabrics in your blocks. Create blocks that you would want to receive.

- Trim loose threads, but do not trim the blocks you'll be swapping unless agreed to by the group.

- Check your blocks for accuracy. A 6½" block needs to measure 6½". Be sure you're using an accurate ¼" seam allowance.

- Follow the pattern and press the seam allowances according to the pattern instructions.

- First and foremost, *be kind*! It's likely that you'll not be thrilled with all the blocks you receive in your exchange. Accept them in the spirit they were given. In the long run, they'll each fit into your quilt and the result will be beautiful.

Sixteen Patch

Starting with a quick and easy block is perfect for a new exchange group. The rules will be easy for participants to follow. The Sixteen Patch block is ideal, and we decided to piece ours in a color combination with wide appeal—red, white, and blue. We used navy reproduction prints and off-white and cream shirtings for ours, but any color scheme would be great.

Exchanging the Blocks

This exchange is for 10 participants.

Each participant will make two sets of 10 blocks each (20 total). All the blocks in one set will be identical for easy cutting and assembly. All the blocks in the second set will match one another but be different from the first set.

After the blocks are made, place one block from each set in a resealable bag so that you have 10 bags with two different blocks in each bag. After the exchange, each participant will have 20 different Sixteen Patch blocks. Use them to assemble the quilt as instructed on page 12 or create your own unique quilt layout.

Finished quilt: 71" × 85⅛"
Finished block: 10" × 10"

MATERIALS

Yardage is based on 42"-wide fabric.

¾ yard *each* of 2 different light prints for blocks*

¾ yard *each* of 2 different navy prints for blocks*

4⅝ yards of red print for setting squares, setting triangles, outer border, and binding

⅜ yard of navy print for inner border

5¼ yards of fabric for backing

79" × 94" piece of batting

*This yardage is sufficient to make 20 blocks in two sets of 10 for a block exchange. If you are making the quilt by yourself, you'll need 16 navy strips and 16 cream strips, each 3" wide, for the blocks.

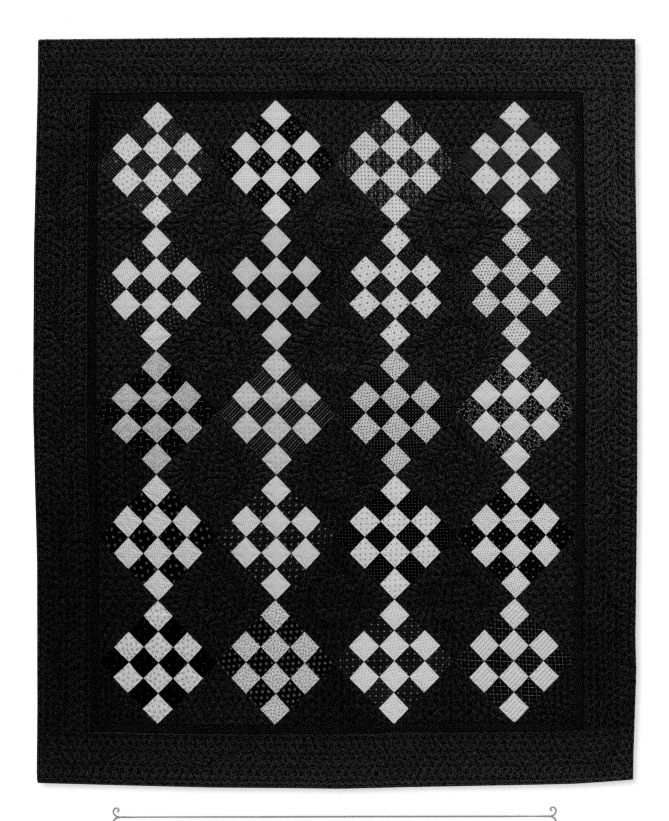

Pieced by Mary Ellen Robison and Paula Barnes;
quilted by Marcella Pickett

CUTTING

You'll need 20 blocks to complete the featured quilt. Cutting is given for 10 blocks at a time; the number of pieces listed in parentheses provides the total amount needed to make 20 blocks. (See "Exchanging the Blocks" on page 9.) For greater ease in piecing the blocks, keep the pieces for each block grouped together. All measurements include ¼" seam allowances.

CUTTING FOR 10 BLOCKS

From *1* light print, cut:

8 strips, 3" × 42" (16 total)

From *1* navy print, cut:

8 strips, 3" × 42" (16 total)

ADDITIONAL CUTTING TO COMPLETE THE QUILT

From the red print, cut:

2 strips, 15½" × 42"; crosscut into:

- 4 squares, 15½" × 15½"; cut the squares into quarters diagonally to yield 16 side triangles (2 are extra)
- 2 squares, 8" × 8"; cut the squares in half diagonally to yield 4 corner triangles

2 strips, 10½" × 42"; crosscut into 6 squares, 10½" × 10½"

9 strips, 2" × 42"

From the remainder of the red print, cut on the *lengthwise* grain:

2 strips, 6½" × 73⅛"

2 strips, 6½" × 71"

6 squares, 10½" × 10½"

From the navy print for inner border, cut:

7 strips, 1½" × 42"

MAKING THE SIXTEEN PATCH BLOCKS

The instructions below are for making four matching strip sets, which will be enough for 10 matching blocks. Then repeat to make 10 more blocks with different fabrics. Press seam allowances in the directions indicated by the arrows.

1 Arrange two matching light and two matching navy 3"-wide strips, alternating them as shown. Sew the strips together to make a strip set measuring 10½" × 42", including seam allowances. Make four strip sets. Cut the strip set into 40 segments, 3" × 10½".

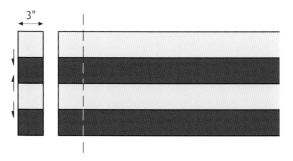

Make 4 strip sets, 10½" × 42".
Cut 40 segments, 3" × 10½".

2 Lay out four segments, orienting them as shown. Join the segments to make a Sixteen Patch block measuring 10½" square, including seam allowances. Make 10 matching blocks.

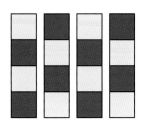 

Make 10 matching
Sixteen Patch blocks,
10½" × 10½".

3 Repeat steps 1 and 2 to make a total of 20 blocks.

ASSEMBLING THE QUILT TOP

1 Referring to the quilt assembly diagram, arrange and sew the blocks and red squares together in diagonal rows, adding the side triangles to the ends of each row as indicated. Join the rows, adding the corner triangles last.

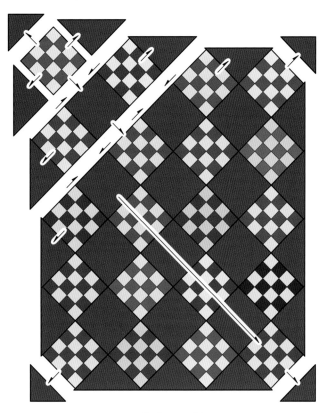

Quilt assembly

2 Trim and square up the quilt top, making sure to leave ¼" beyond the points of all blocks for seam allowances. The quilt top should measure 57" × 71⅛", including seam allowances.

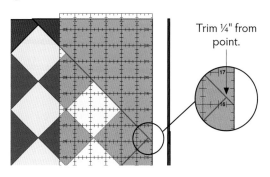

Trim ¼" from point.

3 Join the navy 1½"-wide strips end to end. From the pieced strip, cut two 71⅛"-long strips and two 59"-long strips. Sew the longer strips to opposite sides of the quilt center. Sew the shorter strips to the top and bottom edges. Press the seam allowances toward the navy strips. The quilt top should measure 59" × 73⅛", including seam allowances.

4 Sew the red 73⅛" strips to opposite sides of the quilt center. Sew the red 71"-long strips to the top and bottom edges to complete the quilt top. Press the seam allowances toward the red strips. The quilt top should measure 71" × 85⅛".

FINISHING THE QUILT

For more details on any finishing steps, visit ShopMartingale.com/HowtoQuilt for free downloadable information.

1 Layer the quilt top with batting and backing; baste the layers together.

2 Quilt by hand or machine. The quilt shown is machine quilted with feather wreaths in the setting squares and curved lines in the pieced blocks. A curved grid is stitched in the setting triangles and a continuous feather motif is stitched in the outer border.

3 Make double-fold binding using the red 2"-wide strips. Attach the binding to the quilt.

Crayon Box Nine Patch

A book about block exchanges wouldn't be complete without a Nine Patch block. We thought we'd have a little fun with the fabric selection for this exchange. The leader will select 16 different crayons to signify the color palette of the quilts. The participants then each pick two of them and use those colors when selecting their fabrics. We recommend using small-scale prints and choosing one background fabric that everyone will use. Enjoy our Crayon Box quilt.

Exchanging the Blocks

This exchange is for eight participants.

Each participant will make two sets of 72 blocks each (144 total), one set in one crayon color, the other set in the second color. After the blocks are made, place nine blocks from each set in a resealable bag so that you have eight bags with 18 blocks in each bag. After the exchange, each participant will have 144 Nine Patch blocks in 16 different colors. Use them to assemble the quilt as instructed on page 17 or create your own unique quilt layout.

Finished quilt: 97¼" × 97¼"
Finished block: 4½" × 4½"

MATERIALS

Yardage is based on 42"-wide fabric.

5⅞ yards of light print for blocks and setting squares

1 yard *each* of 2 different dark prints for blocks*

¾ yard of blue print for setting triangles

½ yard of brown print for inner border

3¾ yards of beige print for outer border and binding

8⅞ yards of fabric for backing

106" × 106" piece of batting

*Yardage is for making blocks for swapping. If you are making this quilt on your own, you will need ¼ yard each of 16 prints.

CUTTING

You'll need 144 blocks to complete the featured quilt. Cutting is given for nine blocks at a time, which is enough for one set for each participant. The number of pieces in parentheses provides the total amount needed to make 144 blocks. (See "Exchanging the Blocks" on page 13.) For greater ease in piecing the blocks, keep the pieces for each block grouped together. All measurements include ¼" seam allowances.

CUTTING FOR 9 BLOCKS

From the light print, cut:

3 strips, 2" × 42"; cut 1 strip in half (2" x 21") and save half for another strip stet. (40 total; cut 8 in half.)

From *1* dark print, cut:

2 strips, 2" × 42"; cut 1 strip in half (2" x 21"). (32 total; cut 16 in half.)

ADDITIONAL CUTTING TO COMPLETE THE QUILT

Cut the light strips carefully, you will not have any leftover fabric.

From the remainder of the light print, cut:

22 strips, 5" × 42"; crosscut into 169 squares, 5" × 5"

From the blue print, cut:

3 strips, 7⅝" × 42"; crosscut into:

• 12 squares, 7⅝" × 42"; cut the squares into quarters diagonally to yield 48 side triangles

• 2 squares, 4⅛" × 4⅛"; cut the squares in half diagonally to yield 4 corner triangles

From the brown print, cut:

9 strips, 1½" × 42"

From the beige print, cut:

10 strips, 2" × 42"

From the beige print, cut on the *lengthwise* grain:

2 strips, 6½" × 97¼"

2 strips, 6½" × 85¼"

MAKING NINE PATCH BLOCKS

The instructions below are for making nine blocks. Repeat to piece two sets of 72 blocks (144 total). Press seam allowances as indicated by the arrows.

1 Select a set of light and dark strips cut for one colorway. Sew a light strip to each long side of a dark strip to make strip set A measuring 5" × 42", including seam allowances. Cut the strip set into 18 segments, 2" × 5".

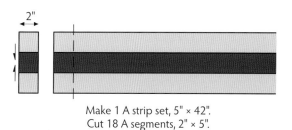

Make 1 A strip set, 5" × 42".
Cut 18 A segments, 2" × 5".

2 Join two dark 2" × 21"strips and a light 2" × 21" strip to make strip set B measuring 5" × 21", including seam allowances. Cut the strip set into nine segments, 2" × 5".

Make 1 B strip set, 5" × 21".
Cut 9 B segments, 2" × 5".

3 Join two A segments and one B segment to make a Nine Patch block measuring 5" square, including seam allowances. You will have enough segments in one pair of strip sets to make nine blocks. Repeat to make seven more matching A and B strip sets to make a total of 72 matching blocks.

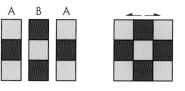

Make 72 Nine Patch blocks,
5" × 5".

4 Repeat steps 1–3 to make 72 Nine Patch blocks in your second colorway, for a total of 144 blocks.

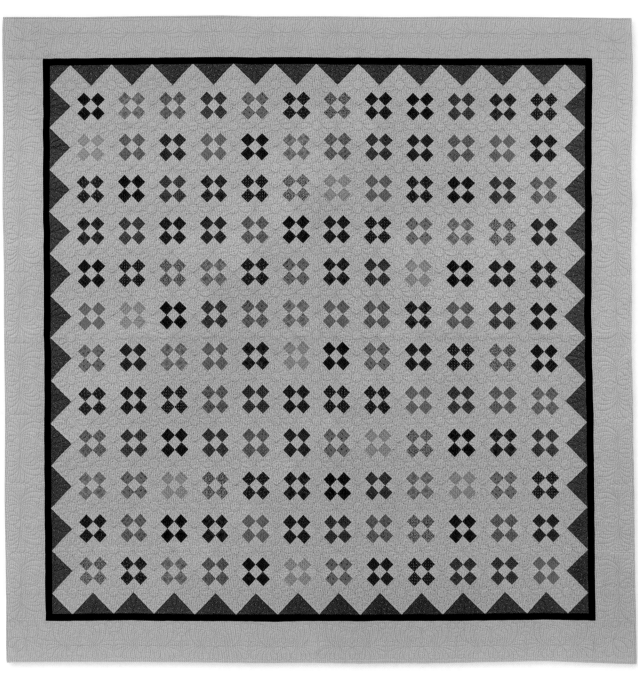

Pieced by Mary Ellen Robison;
quilted by Cathy Peters and Lynn Graham

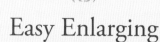

Easy Enlarging

Here's an easy way to enlarge a quilt that's set on point without having to piece more blocks. Simply start and end each row with a setting square instead of a patchwork block. Not only will your quilt be larger but the setting blocks help frame the quilt design. Because the setting squares are a quick way to extend the blocks into a larger quilt top, Paula likes to think of these squares as her "Hamburger Helper" blocks.

ASSEMBLING THE QUILT TOP

1 Referring to the quilt assembly diagram, arrange and sew the blocks and light squares together in diagonal rows, adding the blue side triangles to the ends of each row as indicated. Join the rows, adding the blue corner triangles last.

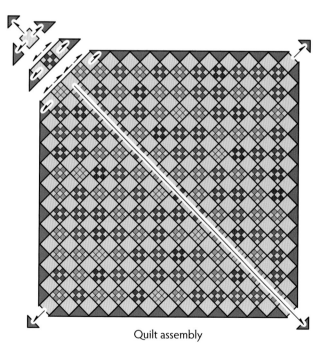

Quilt assembly

2 Trim and square up the quilt top, making sure to leave ¼" beyond the points of all blocks for seam allowances. The quilt top should measure 83¼" square, including seam allowances.

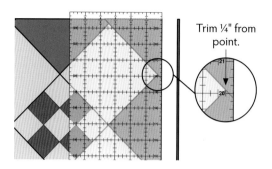

Trim ¼" from point.

3 Join the brown strips end to end. From the pieced strip, cut two 85¼"-long strips and two 83¼"-long strips. Sew the shorter strips to opposite sides of the quilt center. Sew the longer strips to the top and bottom edges. Press the seam allowances toward the brown strips. The quilt top should measure 85¼" square, including seam allowances.

4 Sew the beige 85¼"-long strips to opposite sides of the quilt top. Sew the beige 97¼"-long strips to the top and bottom edges to complete the quilt top. Press the seam allowances toward the outer border. The quilt top should measure 97¼" square.

FINISHING THE QUILT

For more details on any finishing steps, visit ShopMartingale.com/HowtoQuilt for free downloadable information.

1 Layer the quilt top with batting and backing; baste the layers together.

2 Quilt by hand or machine. The quilt shown is machine quilted with feather wreaths in the setting squares and partial feather wreaths in the setting triangles. Overlapping curved lines are stitched in the blocks. A feather motif is stitched in the outer border.

3 Make double-fold binding using the beige 2"-wide strips. Attach the binding to the quilt.

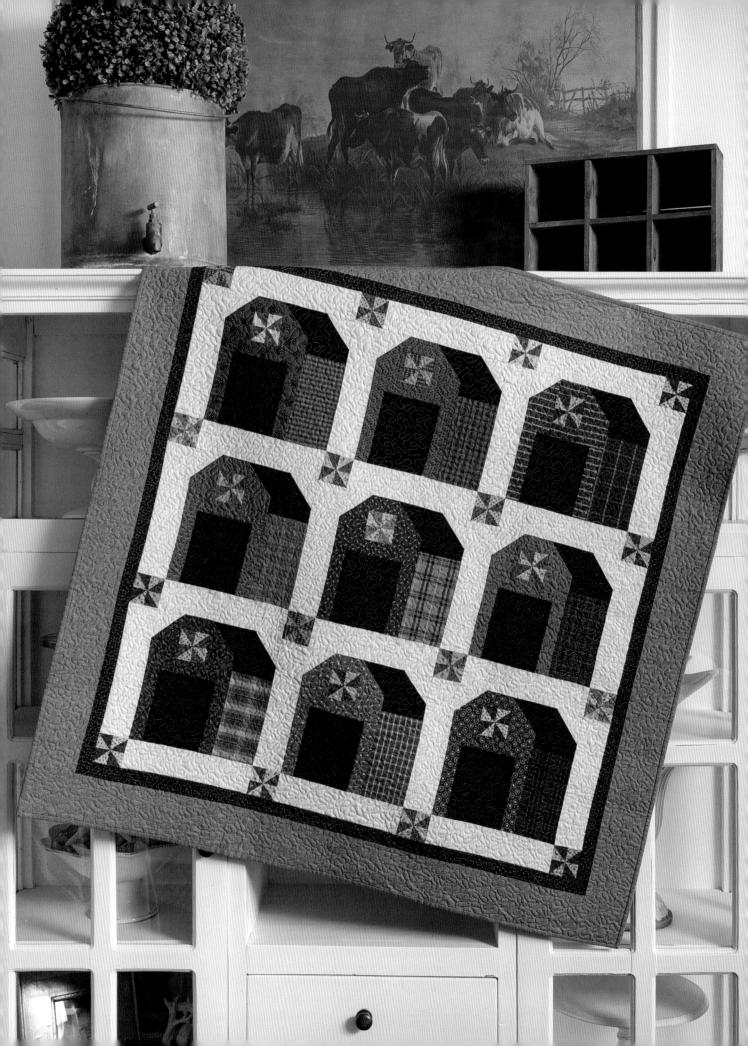

Plaid Barn

Get ready for winter with our cozy little Plaid Barn block exchange. The key to making this exchange work is for everyone to use the same black solid and the same light print for the sky behind the barn. Using the same light print as the sashing gives the quilt a cohesive look. Because of its size, this charmer works up in no time.

Exchanging the Blocks

This exchange is for nine participants.
Each participant will make one set of nine matching Plaid Barn blocks. After the blocks are made, place one block and two pinwheel sashing units in a resealable bag so that you have nine bags. After the exchange, each participant will have nine different Plaid Barn blocks and 18 different pinwheel units. Use them to assemble the quilt as instructed on page 22 or create your own unique quilt layout.

Finished quilt: 43½" × 43½"
Finished block: 9" × 9"

Pieced by Mary Ellen Robison; quilted by Pat Meeks

MATERIALS

Yardage is based on 42"-wide fabric. Yardage is based on making 9 matching blocks for swapping. If you are making the entire quilt yourself and want a variety of barn fronts, you will need 9 assorted fat eighths (9" × 21") or scraps for dark A, 9 assorted fat eighths or scraps for dark B, and 9 assorted plaid fat eighths.

¼ yard of light print for pinwheel units*

¼ yard of dark A print for pinwheel units*

⅝ yard of cream print for blocks and sashing

½ yard of dark B print for blocks

½ yard of black solid for blocks

¼ yard of dark plaid for blocks

¼ yard of black print for inner border

1¾ yards of tan print for outer border and binding

2⅞ yards of fabric for backing

50" × 50" piece of batting

1" finished Star Singles papers (optional)*

*If you use 1" Star Singles papers, you'll need ⅓ yard of each print. See "Using Star Singles" on page 20 before cutting fabrics.

CUTTING

All measurements include ¼" seam allowances.

CUTTING FOR BLOCKS AND SASHING

From the light print, cut:

3 strips, 2" × 42"; crosscut into 54 squares, 2" × 2"

From the dark A print, cut:

3 strips, 2" × 42"; crosscut into 54 squares, 2" × 2"

From the cream print, cut:

8 strips, 2½" × 42"; crosscut into:
- 24 strips, 2½" × 9½"
- 18 squares, 2½" × 2½"

From the dark B print, cut:

3 strips, 2½" × 42"; crosscut into 18 pieces, 2½" × 4½"

4 strips, 1½" × 42"; crosscut into:
- 18 pieces, 1½" × 5½"
- 18 pieces, 1½" × 2½"

From the black solid, cut:

2 strips, 4½" × 42"; crosscut into 9 pieces, 4½" × 5½"

1 strip, 3½" × 42"; crosscut into 9 squares, 3½" × 3½"

1 strip, 2½" × 42"; crosscut into 9 squares, 2½" × 2½"

From the dark plaid, cut:

1 strip, 6½" × 42"; crosscut into 9 pieces, 3½" × 6½"

ADDITIONAL CUTTING TO COMPLETE THE QUILT

From the black print, cut:

4 strips, 1½" × 42"; crosscut into:
- 2 strips, 1½" × 37½"
- 2 strips, 1½" × 35½"

From the tan print, cut:

5 strips, 2" × 42"

From the tan print, cut on the *lengthwise* grain:

2 strips, 3½" × 43½"

2 strips, 3½" × 37½"

Using Star Singles

If you use the 1" Star Singles papers, *do not* cut the 2" squares from the cream and dark A prints. Instead, skip step 1 of "Making the Barn Blocks" below and follow the directions on the package to cut the following pieces.

From the light print, cut:

2 strips, 4½" × 42"; crosscut into 14 squares, 4½" × 4½"

From the dark A print, cut:

2 strips, 4½" × 42"; crosscut into 14 squares, 4½" × 4½"

MAKING THE BARN BLOCKS

Press seam allowances in the directions indicated by the arrows.

1 Referring to "Half-Square-Triangle Units" on page 77, mark the light 2" squares and layer them right sides together with the dark A 2" squares. Sew, cut, press, and trim to 1½" square. Make 108 half-square-triangle units.

Make 108 units.

2 Lay out four half-square-triangle units in two rows of two, rotating the units to form a pinwheel. Sew the units into rows. Join the rows to make a pinwheel unit measuring 2½" square, including seam allowances. Make 27 units. (If you are not participating in the block exchange, you'll have two pinwheel units left over.)

Make 27 units,
2½" × 2½".

3 Draw a diagonal line from corner to corner on the wrong side of the cream squares. Place a marked square on one end of a dark B 2½" × 4½" piece, right sides together, making sure to orient the line as shown. Sew on the marked line. Trim the excess corner fabric ¼" from the stitched line. Make nine units measuring 2½" × 4½", including seam allowances. Set aside the remaining marked squares for step 6.

Make 9 units,
2½" × 4½".

4 Draw a diagonal line from corner to corner on the wrong side of the black solid 2½" squares. Place a marked square on one end of a dark B 2½" × 4½" piece, right sides together, making sure to orient the line as shown. Sew on the marked line. Trim the excess corner fabric ¼" from the stitched line. Make nine units measuring 2½" × 4½", including seam allowances.

Make 9 units,
2½" × 4½".

5 Lay out one unit from step 3, one pinwheel unit, two dark B 1½" × 2½" pieces, and one unit from step 4, according to the diagram. Sew the pieces to the pinwheel unit. Press. Add the remaining units to make a barn-top unit. Make nine units measuring 4½" × 6½", including seam allowances.

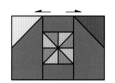

Make 9 units,
4½" × 6½".

6 Place a marked cream square from step 3 on one corner of a black solid 3½" square, right sides together. Sew on the marked line. Trim the excess corner fabric ¼" from the stitched line. Make nine units measuring 3½" square, including seam allowances.

Make 9 units,
3½" × 3½".

7 Sew a unit from step 6 to one end of a dark plaid piece to make a side unit. Make nine units measuring 3½" × 9½", including seam allowances.

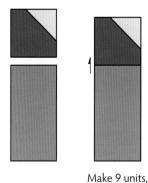

Make 9 units,
3½" × 9½".

8 Sew dark B 1½" × 5½" pieces to opposite sides of a black solid 4½" × 5½" piece to make a barn-door unit. Make nine units measuring 5½" × 6½", including seam allowances.

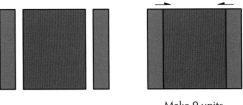

Make 9 units,
5½" × 6½".

9 Join a barn-top and a barn-door unit. Sew a side unit to the right edge to make a Barn block. Make nine blocks measuring 9½" square, including seam allowances.

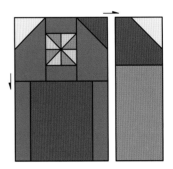

Make 9 Barn blocks,
9½" × 9½".

ASSEMBLING THE QUILT TOP

1 Join four pinwheel units and three cream strips to make a sashing row. Make four rows measuring 2½" × 35½", including seam allowances.

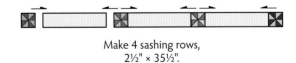

Make 4 sashing rows,
2½" × 35½".

2 Join four cream strips and three blocks to make a block row. Make three rows measuring 9½" × 35½", including seam allowances.

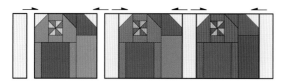

Make 3 block rows,
9½" × 35½".

3 Join the sashing rows and block rows, alternating them as shown in the quilt assembly diagram below. The quilt top should measure 35½" square, including seam allowances.

4 Sew the black print 35½"-long strips to opposite sides of the quilt top. Sew the black print 37½"-long strips to the top and bottom edges. The quilt top should measure 37½" square, including seam allowances.

5 Sew the tan 37½"-long strips to opposite sides of the quilt top. Sew the tan 43½"-long strips to the top and bottom edges to complete the quilt top. The quilt top should measure 43½" square.

FINISHING THE QUILT

For more details on any finishing steps, visit ShopMartingale.com/HowtoQuilt for free downloadable information.

1 Layer the quilt top with batting and backing; baste the layers together.

2 Quilt by hand or machine. The quilt shown is machine quilted with an allover meandering motif.

3 Make double-fold binding using the tan 2"-wide strips. Attach the binding to the quilt.

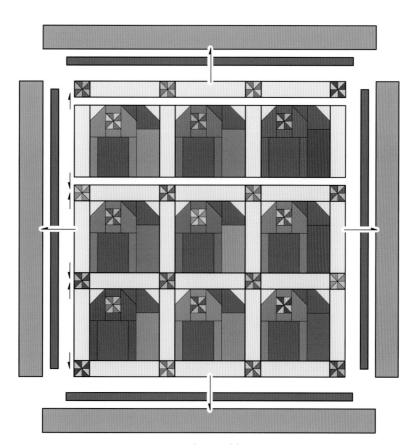

Quilt assembly

Plaid Barn

Friendship Star

Living in Southern states leaves us both wishing for autumn and its beautiful colors. The Friendship Star block is a perfect choice for fall fabrics, but it would be just as cute in a patriotic palette or in Christmas or springtime colors. We designed the exchange to provide the 36 blocks and the half-square-triangle units needed for a pieced border.

Exchanging the Blocks

This exchange is for six participants. Each participant will make six sets of six blocks each (36 total). After the blocks are made, place one block and two half-square-triangle units from each set in a resealable bag so that you have six bags with six different blocks and 12 triangle units in each bag. You'll have four half-square-triangle units from each set left over (24 total). Distribute these evenly (sort of like dealing from a deck of cards) so that each bag has a total of 16 half-square-triangle units. After the exchange, each participant will have 36 different Friendship Star blocks and 96 half-square-triangle units. Use them to assemble the quilt as instructed on page 28 or create your own unique quilt layout.

Finished quilt: 47½" × 47½"
Finished block: 4½" × 4½"

MATERIALS

Yardage is based on 42"-wide fabric.

⅓ yard *each* of 6 assorted light and medium prints (referred to collectively as "light") for blocks and triangle border

¼ yard *each* of 6 assorted dark prints for blocks and triangle border

⅝ yard of olive print for sashing and border 1

⅓ yard of tan print for cornerstones and border 2

1⅛ yards of green print for border 4 and binding

3 yards of fabric for backing

54" × 54" piece of batting

1½" finished Star Singles papers (optional)*

*See "Using Star Singles" on page 26 before cutting fabrics.

CUTTING

You'll need 36 blocks to complete the featured quilt. Cutting is given for one block at a time; the number of pieces listed in parentheses provides the total amount needed to make 36 blocks. (See "Exchanging the Blocks" on page 25.) For greater ease in piecing the blocks, keep the pieces for each block grouped together. All measurements include ¼" seam allowances.

CUTTING FOR 1 BLOCK

From *1* light print, cut:

2 squares, 2½" × 2½" (72 total)

4 squares, 2" × 2" (144 total)

From *1* dark print, cut:

2 squares, 2½" × 2½" (72 total)

1 square, 2" × 2" (36 total)

ADDITIONAL CUTTING TO COMPLETE THE QUILT

From the remainder of the light prints, cut a *total* of:

48 squares, 2½" × 2½"

From the remainder of the dark prints, cut a *total* of:

48 squares, 2½" × 2½"

From the olive print, cut:

13 strips, 1½" × 42"; crosscut into:

• 2 strips, 1½" × 34½"

• 2 strips, 1½" × 32½"

• 60 strips, 1½" × 5"

From the tan print, cut:

5 strips, 1½" × 42"; crosscut into:

• 2 strips, 1½" × 36½"

• 2 strips, 1½" × 34½"

• 25 squares, 1½" × 1½"

4 squares, 2" × 2"

From the green print, cut:

5 strips, 4½" × 42"

5 strips, 2" × 42"

Using Star Singles

If you use the 1½" Star Singles papers, *do not* cut the 2½" squares from the light and dark prints. Instead, skip step 1 of "Making the Friendship Star Blocks" below and step 3 of "Adding the Borders" on page 28 and follow the directions on the package to cut the following pieces.

From *each* of the light prints, cut:

5 squares, 5½" × 5½" (30 total)

From *each* of the dark prints, cut:

5 squares, 5½" × 5½" (30 total)

MAKING THE FRIENDSHIP STAR BLOCKS

The instructions below are for making one block. Repeat to piece six sets of six matching blocks each (36 total). Press seam allowances in the directions indicated by the arrows.

1 Select a set of pieces cut for one block. Referring to "Half-Square-Triangle Units" on page 77, mark the light 2½" squares and layer them right sides together with the dark 2½" squares. Sew, cut, press, and trim to 2" square. Make four half-square-triangle units.

Make 4 units.

Pieced by Mary Ellen Robison; quilted by Pat Meeks

Friendship Star

ASSEMBLING THE QUILT TOP

1 Join six blocks and five olive 1½" × 5" strips to make a block row. Make six rows measuring 5" × 32½", including seam allowances.

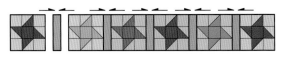

Make 6 block rows,
5" × 32½".

2 Join six olive 1½" × 5" strips and five tan 1½" squares to make a sashing row. Make five rows measuring 2" × 32½", including seam allowances.

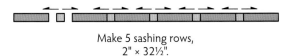

Make 5 sashing rows,
2" × 32½".

3 Join the block rows and sashing rows, alternating them as shown in the quilt assembly diagram on page 29. The quilt top should measure 32½" square, including seam allowances.

ADDING THE BORDERS

1 Sew the olive 32½"-long strips to opposite sides of the quilt top. Sew the olive 34½"-long strips to the top and bottom edges. The quilt top should measure 34½" square, including seam allowances.

2 Sew the tan 34½"-long strips to opposite sides of the quilt top. Sew the tan 36½"-long strips to the top and bottom edges. The quilt top should measure 36½" square, including seam allowances.

3 To make the half-square-triangle units, mark the remaining light 2½" squares and layer them right sides together with the dark 2½" squares. Sew, cut, press, and trim to 2" square. Make 96 half-square-triangle units.

Make 96 units.

2 Lay out four light 2" squares, the four matching units from step 1, and one dark 2" square that matches the triangle units in three rows. Sew the squares and units into rows. Join the rows to make a Friendship Star block measuring 5" square, including seam allowances.

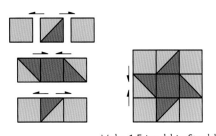

Make 1 Friendship Star block,
5" × 5".

3 Repeat steps 1 and 2 to make six sets of six matching blocks, for 36 blocks total.

Quilt Club

4 Join 24 half-square-triangle units, with 12 units pointing in one direction and 12 units pointing in the opposite direction, to make a side border measuring 2" × 36½", including seam allowances. Make two. Make two more borders in the same way, and add a tan 2" square to each end. The top and bottom borders should measure 2" × 39½", including seam allowances.

Make 2 side borders,
2" × 36½".

Make 2 top/bottom borders,
2" × 39½".

5 Sew the triangle borders to opposite sides of the quilt top and then to the top and bottom edges. The quilt top should measure 39½" square, including seam allowances.

6 Join the green 4½"-wide strips end to end. From the pieced strip, cut two 47½"-long strips and two 39½"-long strips. Sew the shorter strips to opposite sides of the quilt center. Sew the longer strips to the top and bottom edges to complete the quilt top. The quilt top should measure 47½" square.

FINISHING THE QUILT

For more details on any finishing steps, visit ShopMartingale.com/HowtoQuilt for free downloadable information.

1 Layer the quilt top with batting and backing; baste the layers together.

2 Quilt by hand or machine. The quilt shown is machine quilted with an allover meandering motif.

3 Make double-fold binding using the green 2"-wide strips. Attach the binding to the quilt.

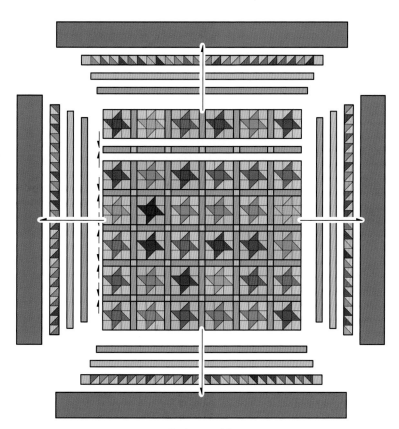

Quilt assembly

Friendship Star

Scrappy Star

Everyone loves a scrappy quilt, and if it has scrappy stars, it's even better. We used one light and four dark prints for each block. Sometimes it's fun if an exchange group swaps more than just the blocks. For this quilt, consider exchanging sashing strips and cornerstones too for the ultimate scrap quilt. All you'll need to add are border fabrics for a finished quilt.

Exchanging the Blocks

This exchange is for 12 participants. Each participant will make three sets of 12 matching blocks each (36 total). Distribute the light 2" × 6½" strips and dark 2" squares evenly into 12 stacks. After the blocks are made, place one block from each set in a resealable bag so that you have 12 bags with three blocks, seven assorted light strips, and four assorted dark squares in each bag. After the exchange, each participant will have 36 different Scrappy Star blocks, 84 sashing strips, and 48 cornerstones. Use them to assemble the quilt as instructed on page 34 or create your own unique quilt layout.

Finished quilt: 57" × 57"

Finished block: 6" × 6"

MATERIALS

Yardage is based on 42"-wide fabric.

¾ yard *each* of 3 assorted light prints for blocks and sashing*

⅓ yard *each* of 3 assorted dark A prints for blocks and cornerstones*

⅓ yard *each* of 3 assorted dark B prints for blocks and cornerstones*

½ yard *each* of 3 assorted dark C prints for blocks and cornerstones*

¼ yard *each* of 3 assorted dark D prints for blocks and cornerstones*

¾ yard of charcoal print for inner border and binding

1¾ yards of tan print for outer border

3½ yards of fabric for backing

63" × 63" piece of batting

2" finished Star Singles papers (optional)**

*Yardage is for making blocks for swapping. If you are making this quilt on your own, you'll need 2⅜ yards total of assorted light scraps and 3½ yards total of assorted dark scraps.

**See "Using Star Singles" on page 33 before cutting fabrics.

Pieced by Mary Ellen Robison; quilted by Sarabeth Rebe

Quilt Club

Using Star Singles

If you use the 2" Star Singles papers, *do not* cut the 3¼" squares from the light and dark A prints. Instead, skip step 1 of "Making the Scrappy Star Blocks" below right and follow the directions on the package to cut the following pieces.

From *each* of the light prints, cut:
6 squares, 6½" × 6½" (18 total)

From *each* of the dark A prints, cut:
6 squares, 6½" × 6½" (18 total)

CUTTING

You'll need 36 blocks to complete the featured quilt. Cutting is given for one block at a time; the number of pieces listed in parentheses provides the total amount needed to make 36 blocks. (See "Exchanging the Blocks" on page 31.) For greater ease in piecing the blocks, keep the pieces for each block grouped together. All measurements include ¼" seam allowances.

CUTTING FOR 1 BLOCK

From *1* light print, cut:
1 square, 3½" × 3½" (36 total); cut the square into quarters diagonally to yield 4 triangles (144 total)
2 squares, 3¼" × 3¼" (72 total)

From *each* of the dark A prints, cut:
2 squares, 3¼" × 3¼" (72 total)

From *each* of the dark B prints, cut:
1 square, 3½" × 3½" (36 total); cut the square into quarters diagonally to yield 4 triangles (144 total)

From *each* of the dark C prints, cut:
2 squares, 3½" × 3½" (72 total); cut the square in half diagonally to yield 4 triangles (144 total)

From *each* of the dark D prints, cut:
1 square, 2½" × 2½" (36 total)

ADDITIONAL CUTTING TO COMPLETE THE QUILT

From the remaining light prints, cut a *total* of:
84 strips, 2" × 6½"

From the remaining dark prints, cut a *total* of:
49 squares, 2" × 2"

From the charcoal print, cut:
5 strips, 1½" × 42"
6 strips, 2" × 42"

From the tan print, cut on the *lengthwise* grain:
2 strips, 4½" × 57"
2 strips, 4½" × 49"

MAKING THE SCRAPPY STAR BLOCKS

The instructions below are for making one block. Repeat to piece three sets of 12 blocks (36 total). Press seam allowances in the directions indicated by the arrows.

1 Select a set of pieces cut for one block. Referring to "Half-Square-Triangle Units" on page 77, mark the light 3¼" squares and layer them right sides together with the dark A 3¼" squares. Sew, cut, press, and trim to 2½" square. Make four half-square-triangle units.

Make 4 units.

2 Sew a light triangle to one short side of a dark B triangle. Add a dark C triangle, centering it on the pieced triangle, to make a star-point unit. The C triangles are cut oversized and will not match the point. Refer to "Trimming Star-Point Units" at right to trim the units to 2½" square. Make four units.

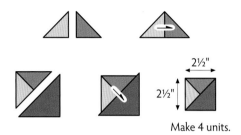

Make 4 units.

3 Lay out four matching half-square-triangle units, four matching star-point units, and one dark D 2½" square in three rows, rotating the units as shown. Sew the pieces into rows. Join the rows to make a Scrappy Star block measuring 6½" square, including seam allowances.

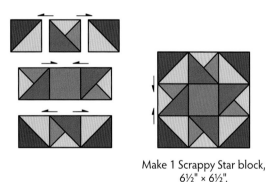

Make 1 Scrappy Star block,
6½" × 6½".

4 Repeat steps 1–3 to make a total of 36 blocks.

ASSEMBLING THE QUILT TOP

1 Join seven assorted dark 2" squares and six assorted light 2" × 6½" strips to make a sashing row. Make seven rows measuring 2" × 47", including seam allowances.

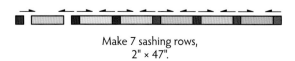

Make 7 sashing rows,
2" × 47".

Trimming Star-Point Units

We like to make star-point units oversized and trim them after sewing. This guarantees that the units will be the exact size needed.

1 Place a square ruler on top of the unit, aligning the 45° line of the ruler with the diagonal seamline of the star-point unit. Divide the desired trimmed size of the unit by two and make sure those lines of the ruler meet at the center of the unit. For the 2½" unfinished unit, place the 1¼" lines at the center of the unit. The 2½" lines of the ruler should line up with the opposite diagonal seam of the star-point unit.

2 Trim the unit along the top and right edges of the ruler.

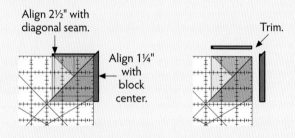

Align 2½" with diagonal seam.

Align 1¼" with block center.

Trim.

3 Rotate the unit so that the newly trimmed sides align with the 2½" lines of the ruler and the 45° line of the ruler is aligned with the diagonal seamline of the star-point unit. The 1¼" lines should meet in the center of the unit as in step 1.

4 Trim the unit along the top and right edges of the ruler. You now have a perfect star-point unit.

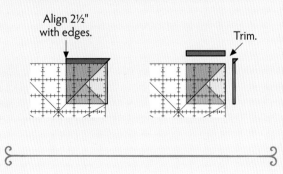

Align 2½" with edges.

Trim.

Quilt Club

2 Join seven assorted light 2" × 6½" strips and six blocks to make a block row. Make six rows measuring 6½" × 47", including seam allowances.

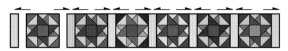

Make 6 block rows,
6½" × 47".

3 Join the block rows and sashing rows, alternating them as shown in the quilt assembly diagram below. The quilt top should measure 47" square, including seam allowances.

4 Join the charcoal strips end to end. From the pieced strip, cut two 49"-long strips and two 47"-long strips. Sew the shorter strips to opposite sides of the quilt center. Sew the longer strips to the top and bottom edges. The quilt top should measure 49" square, including seam allowances.

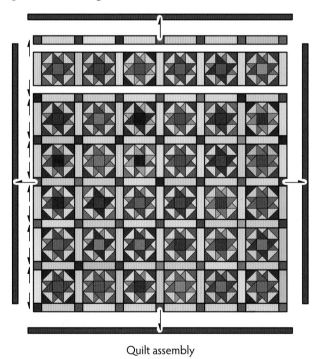

Quilt assembly

5 Sew the tan 49"-long strips to opposite sides of the quilt center. Sew the tan 57"-long strips to the top and bottom edges to complete the quilt top. Press all seam allowances toward the outer border. The quilt top should measure 57" square.

FINISHING THE QUILT

For more details on any finishing steps, visit ShopMartingale.com/HowtoQuilt for free downloadable information.

1 Layer the quilt top with batting and backing; baste the layers together.

2 Quilt by hand or machine. The quilt shown is machine quilted with an allover design of swirls and feathers in the quilt center. Curved lines and a feather motif are stitched in the outer border.

3 Make double-fold binding using the charcoal 2"-wide strips. Attach the binding to the quilt.

Scrappy Star

Hourglass and Double Four Patch

Sometimes a collection of fabric or a specific colorway will just call your name and basically beg to be a quilt. For this exchange, we went with reds, taupes, pinks, and creamy shirtings and exchanged both the Double Four Patch blocks and the Hourglass blocks. Add your choice of borders and you'll have a beautiful quilt.

Exchanging the Blocks

This exchange is for seven participants.

Each participant will make four sets of 14 Hourglass blocks (56 total), four sets of seven light Double Four Patch blocks (28 total), and four sets of seven dark Double Four Patch blocks (28 total). After the blocks are made, from each set place two Hourglass blocks, one light Double Four Patch block, and one dark Double Four Patch block in a resealable bag. You should have seven bags with eight Hourglass blocks, one light Double Four Patch block, and one dark Double Four Patch block in each bag. After the exchange, each participant will have 56 different Double Four Patch blocks and 28 sets of two matching Hourglass blocks. Use them to assemble the quilt as instructed on page 41 or create your own unique quilt layout.

Finished quilt: 95½" × 103½"
Finished block: 8" × 8"

MATERIALS

Yardage is based on 42"-wide fabric.

⅞ yard *each* of 4 assorted light A prints for blocks*

⅞ yard *each* of 4 assorted dark A prints for blocks*

⅓ yard *each* of 4 assorted light B prints for blocks*

⅓ yard *each* of 4 assorted dark B prints for blocks*

⅝ yard of cream print for inner border

3¾ yards of rose print for outer border and binding

8¾ yards of fabric for backing

104" × 112" piece of batting

*Yardage is for making blocks for swapping. If you are making this quilt on your own, you will need 5⅛ yards total of assorted light scraps and 5⅛ yards total of assorted dark scraps.

CUTTING

You'll need 56 Hourglass blocks and 56 Double Four Patch blocks to complete the featured quilt. Cutting is given for two Hourglass and four Double Four Patch blocks at a time; the number of pieces listed in parentheses provides the total amount needed to make 56 Hourglass blocks and 56 Double Four Patch blocks. (See "Exchanging the Blocks" on page 37.) For greater ease in piecing the blocks, keep the pieces for each block grouped together. All measurements include ¼" seam allowances.

CUTTING FOR 2 HOURGLASS BLOCKS

From *1* light A print, cut:
1 square, 9½" × 9½" (28 total); cut the square into quarters diagonally to yield 4 triangles (112 total)

From *1* dark A print, cut:
1 square, 9½" × 9½" (28 total); cut the square into quarters diagonally to yield 4 triangles (112 total)

CUTTING FOR 4 DOUBLE FOUR PATCH BLOCKS

From *1* light A print, cut:
4 squares, 4½" × 4½" (56 total)

From *1* dark A print, cut:
4 squares, 4½" × 4½" (56 total)

From *1* light B print, cut:
1 strip, 2½" × 42" (14 total)

From *1* dark B print, cut:
1 strip, 2½" × 42" (14 total)

Be Prepared

When cutting fabric pieces for a quilt, you'll find it easier to stay organized if you place the pieces in labeled resealable bags. When you're ready to piece the blocks, you can simply reach into the bags for the correct-sized pieces.

ADDITIONAL CUTTING TO COMPLETE THE QUILT

From the cream print, cut:
9 strips, 2" × 42"

From the rose print, cut:
11 strips, 2" × 42"

From the rose print, cut on the *lengthwise* grain:
2 strips, 6½" × 95½"
2 strips, 6½" × 91½"

MAKING THE HOURGLASS BLOCKS

The instructions below are for making one block. Repeat to piece four sets of 14 matching blocks (56 total). Press seam allowances as indicated by arrows.

1 Sew a light A and dark A triangle together as shown. Make two identical units; sew them together to make an Hourglass block. Make 56 blocks.

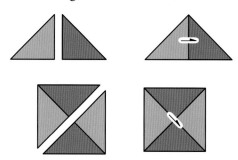

Make 56 Hourglass blocks.

2 Align the 45° line of a square ruler with the diagonal seamline on an Hourglass block as shown, making sure the 4¼" lines meet in the center of the block. Make sure the 8½" lines on the ruler meet on the diagonal seamlines. Trim along the top and right edges of the ruler.

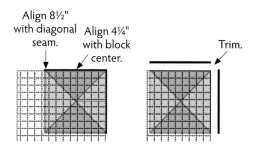

Align 8½" with diagonal seam.   Align 4¼" with block center.   Trim.

Pieced by Mary Ellen Robison and Paula Barnes;
quilted by Sharon Dixon

Hourglass and Double Four Patch

3 Rotate the block 180° so that you can trim the other sides. Align the 45° line of the ruler with the diagonal seamline of the block, making sure the 4¼" lines meet in the center. The 8½" lines on the ruler should align with the previously cut edges. Trim along the top and right sides of the square ruler. Repeat the trimming steps for each of the Hourglass blocks. The blocks should measure 8½" square, including seam allowances.

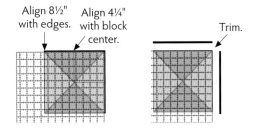

Align 8½" with edges.   Align 4¼" with block center.   Trim.

MAKING 4 DOUBLE FOUR PATCH BLOCKS

The instructions below are for making two light and two dark blocks (four total). Repeat to piece four sets of seven light blocks (28 total) and four sets of seven dark blocks (28 total).

1 Select a set of pieces cut for four blocks. Sew a light B strip to the long side of a dark B strip to make a strip set measuring 4½" × 42", including seam allowances. Cut the strip sets into 16 segments, 2½" × 4½". *Cut the strip set carefully; you will not have any leftover fabric.*

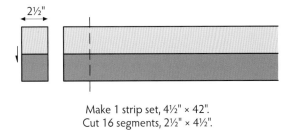

2½"

Make 1 strip set, 4½" × 42".
Cut 16 segments, 2½" × 4½".

2 Join two segments to make a four-patch unit measuring 4½" square, including seam allowances. Make four units.

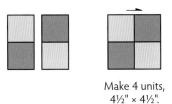

Make 4 units,
4½" × 4½".

3 Lay out two four-patch units and two light A squares in two rows, noting the orientation of the units. Sew the squares and units into rows. Join the rows to make a light Double Four Patch block measuring 8½" square, including seam allowances. Make two blocks.

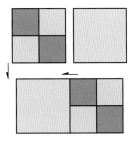

Make 2 light Double Four Patch blocks,
8½" × 8½".

4 Lay out two four-patch units and two dark A squares in two rows, noting the orientation of the units. Sew the squares and units into rows. Join the rows to make a dark Double Four Patch block measuring 8½" square, including seam allowances. Make two blocks.

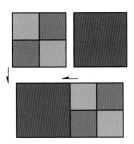

Make 2 dark Double Four Patch blocks,
8½" × 8½".

5 Repeat the steps to make six more strip sets and a total of 28 light blocks and 28 dark blocks (56 total).

ASSEMBLING THE QUILT TOP

1 Lay out the blocks in 11 rows of 10 blocks each, alternating the Hourglass and Double Four Patch blocks as shown in the quilt assembly diagram below. The Double Four Patch blocks should form diagonal lines of light and dark squares across the quilt top. Sew the blocks into rows. Join the rows to make the quilt-top center, which should measure 80½" × 88½", including seam allowances. (If you're not participating in the block exchange, you'll have one Hourglass block and one Double Four Patch block left over.)

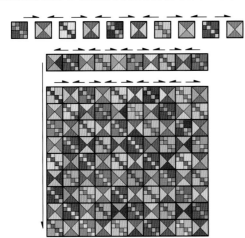

Quilt assembly

2 Join the cream strips end to end. From the pieced strip, cut two 88½"-long strips and two 83½"-long strips. Sew the longer strips to opposite sides of the quilt center. Sew the shorter strips to the top and bottom edges. Press all seam allowances toward the cream strips. The quilt top should measure 83½" × 91½", including seam allowances.

3 Sew the rose 91½"-long strips to opposite sides of the quilt top. Sew the rose 95½"-long strips to the top and bottom edges to complete the quilt top. Press all seam allowances toward the outer border. The quilt top should measure 95½" × 103½".

FINISHING THE QUILT

For more details on any finishing steps, visit ShopMartingale.com/HowtoQuilt for free downloadable information.

1 Layer the quilt top with batting and backing; baste the layers together.

2 Quilt by hand or machine. The quilt shown is machine quilted with an allover feather motif.

3 Make double-fold binding using the rose 2"-wide strips. Attach the binding to the quilt.

Mosaic

Not all exchanges need to result in a finished quilt block. By exchanging half-square-triangle units, the sky's the limit. Both Mosaic and Little Sawtooth (page 55) are made with the same size of triangle units, but the quilts look remarkably different.

Exchanging the Half-Square-Triangle Units

This exchange is for 10 participants. Each participant will make 10 sets of 80 half-square-triangle units each (800 total). After making the units, place eight half-square-triangle units from each set in a resealable bag so that you have 10 bags with 80 different units in each bag. After the exchange, each participant will have an assortment of 800 half-square-triangle units. Use them to make Mosaic blocks and assemble the quilt as instructed on page 47 or create your own unique blocks and quilt layout.

Finished quilt: 95½" × 95½"
Finished block: 8" × 8"

MATERIALS

Yardage is based on 42"-wide fabric.

½ yard *each* of 10 assorted light prints for half-square-triangle units*

½ yard *each* of 10 assorted dark prints for half-square-triangle units*

2⅝ yards of cream print for setting blocks and inner border

4¾ yards of blue print for setting blocks, outer border, and binding

8¾ yards of fabric for backing

104" × 104" piece of batting

2" finished Star Singles papers (optional)**

*If you want to use scraps, you'll need 100 light and 100 dark 7" squares.

**See "Using Star Singles" on page 45 before cutting fabrics.

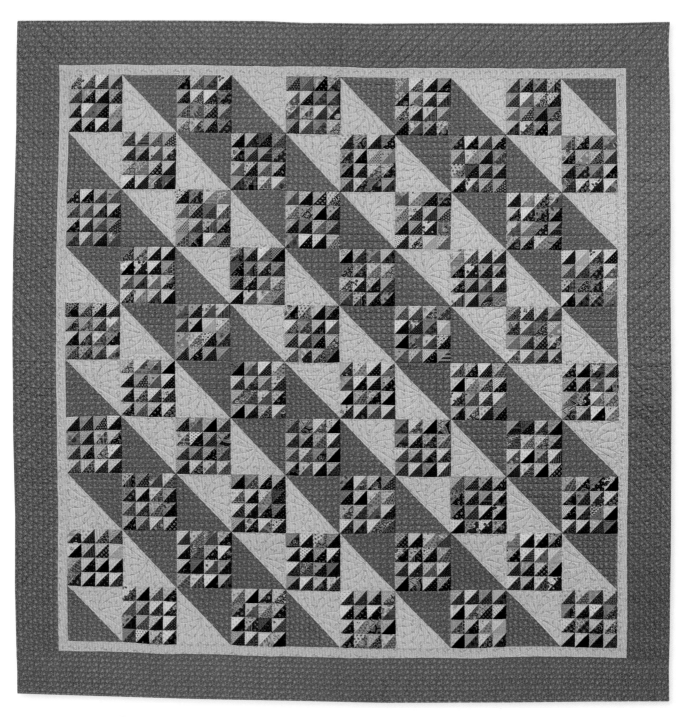

Pieced by Mary Ellen Robison; quilted by Marcella Pickett

Quilt Club

Using Star Singles

If you use the 2" Star Singles papers, *do not* cut the 3" squares from the light and dark prints. Instead, skip "Making the Half-Square-Triangle Units" below right and follow the directions on the package to cut the following pieces.

From *each* of the assorted light prints, cut:
2 strips, 6½" × 42"; crosscut into 10 squares, 6½" × 6½" (100 total)

From *each* of the assorted dark prints, cut:
2 strips, 6½" × 42"; crosscut into 10 squares, 6½" × 6½" (100 total)

CUTTING

All measurements include ¼" seam allowances.

CUTTING FOR HALF-SQUARE-TRIANGLE UNITS

From *each* of the assorted light prints, cut:
4 strips, 3" × 42"; crosscut into 40 squares, 3" × 3" (400 total)

From *each* of the assorted dark prints, cut:
4 strips, 3" × 42"; crosscut into 40 squares, 3" × 3" (400 total)

ADDITIONAL CUTTING TO COMPLETE THE QUILT

From the cream print, cut
7 strips, 9¼" × 42"; crosscut into 25 squares, 9¼" × 9¼"

9 strips, 2" × 42"

From the blue print, cut:
7 strips, 9¼" × 42"; crosscut into 25 squares, 9¼" × 9¼"

10 strips, 6½" × 42"

10 strips, 2" × 42"

MAKING THE HALF-SQUARE-TRIANGLE UNITS

Press seam allowances in the directions indicated by the arrows. Referring to "Half-Square-Triangle Units" on page 77, mark the light 3" squares and layer them right sides together with the dark 3" squares. Sew, cut, press, and trim to 2½" square. Make 10 sets of 80 matching half-square-triangle units (800 total).

Make 10 sets of 80 matching units.

MAKING THE BLOCKS

1 Lay out 16 assorted half-square-triangle units in four rows of four, orienting the units as shown. Sew the units into rows. Join the rows to make a Mosaic block measuring 8½" square, including seam allowances. Make 50 blocks.

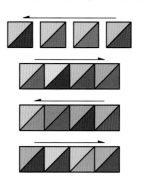

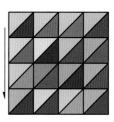

Make 50 Mosaic blocks, 8½" × 8½".

2 Referring to "Half-Square-Triangle Units," mark the cream squares and layer them right sides together with the blue squares. Sew, cut, press, and trim to 8½" square. Make 50 setting blocks.

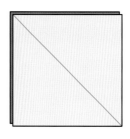

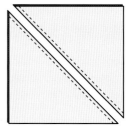

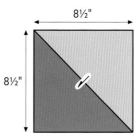

Make 50 setting blocks.

ASSEMBLING THE QUILT TOP

1 Lay out the Mosaic and setting blocks in 10 rows of 10 blocks each, alternating them and noting the orientation of the setting blocks. In the quilt shown, the diagonal in the setting squares slants from top left to bottom right. The diagonal slants in the opposite direction on the little triangles in the Mosaic blocks. Sew the blocks into rows. Join the rows to make the quilt-top center, which should measure 80½" square, including seam allowances.

2 Join the cream 2"-wide strips end to end. From the pieced strip, cut two 83½"-long strips and two 80½"-long strips. Sew the shorter strips to opposite sides of the quilt center. Sew the longer strips to the top and bottom edges. The quilt top should measure 83½" square, including seam allowances.

3 Join the blue 6½"-wide strips end to end. From the pieced strip, cut two 95½"-long strips and two 83½"-long strips. Sew the shorter strips to opposite sides of the quilt top. Sew the longer strips to the top and bottom edges to complete the quilt top. The quilt top should measure 95½" square.

FINISHING THE QUILT

For more details on any finishing steps, visit ShopMartingale.com/HowtoQuilt for free downloadable information.

1 Layer the quilt top with batting and backing; baste the layers together.

2 Quilt by hand or machine. The quilt shown is machine quilted with curved lines in the Mosaic blocks. The setting blocks are stitched with half feather wreaths in the cream triangles and crosshatching in the blue triangles. Diagonal lines are stitched in the outer border.

3 Make double-fold binding using the blue 2"-wide strips. Attach the binding to the quilt.

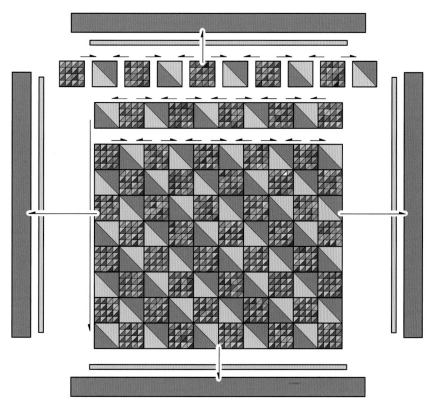

Quilt assembly

Weathervane

Many of our block exchanges are based on using lots of reproduction fabrics. These blocks are then pieced together and become beautiful scrappy quilts. Another interesting way to start pulling together an exchange is by selecting a specific color palette. We chose reds, pinks, golds, tans, and browns for this warm, richly hued quilt.

Exchanging the Blocks

This exchange is for eight participants.
Each participant will make two sets of eight matching Weathervane blocks (16 total). After the blocks are made, place one block from each set in a resealable bag so that you have eight bags with two different blocks in each bag. After the exchange, each participant will have 16 different Weathervane blocks. Use them to assemble the quilt as instructed on page 53 or create your own unique quilt layout.

Finished quilt: 66½" × 66½"
Finished block: 9" × 9"

MATERIALS

Yardage is based on 42"-wide fabric.

⅞ yard *each* of 2 different light prints for Weathervane blocks*

⅓ yard *each* of 2 different dark A prints for Weathervane blocks*

¼ yard *each* of 2 different dark B prints for Weathervane blocks*

⅓ yard *each* of 2 different dark C prints for Weathervane blocks*

¼ yard *each* of 2 different dark D prints for Weathervane blocks*

⅞ yard of tan print for Snowball blocks

1⅓ yards of red print for Snowball blocks and setting triangles

½ yard of beige print for inner border

*Yardage is for making blocks for swapping. If you are making this quilt on your own, you will need 1⅞ yards total of assorted light scraps and 1¾ yards total of assorted dark scraps.

Continued on page 50

Continued from page 49

2⅝ yards of brown print for outer border and binding

4⅛ yards of fabric for backing

73" × 73" piece of batting

1½" finished Star Singles papers (optional)*

*See "Using Star Singles" below before cutting fabrics.

Using Star Singles

If you use the 1½" Star Singles papers, *do not* cut the 2½" squares from the light and dark A prints. Instead, skip step 1 of "Making the Weathervane Blocks" on page 52 and follow the directions on the package to cut the following pieces.

From *each* of the light prints, cut:
2 strips, 5½" × 42"; crosscut into 8 squares, 5½" × 5½" (16 total)

From *each* of the dark A prints, cut:
2 strips, 5½" × 42"; crosscut into 8 squares, 5½" × 5½" (16 total)

CUTTING

You'll need 16 blocks to complete the featured quilt. Cutting is given for one block at a time; the number of pieces listed in parentheses provides the total amount needed to make 16 blocks. (See "Exchanging the Blocks" on page 49.) For greater ease in piecing the blocks, keep the pieces for each block grouped together. All measurements include ¼" seam allowances.

CUTTING FOR 1 WEATHERVANE BLOCK

From *1* light print, cut:
4 squares, 2½" × 2½" (64 total)
12 squares, 2" × 2" (192 total)

From *1* dark A print, cut:
4 squares, 2½" × 2½" (64 total)

From *1* dark B print, cut:
4 squares, 2" × 2" (64 total)

From *1* dark C print, cut:
4 squares, 3½" × 3½" (64 total)

From *1* dark D print, cut:
1 square, 3½" × 3½" (16 total)

ADDITIONAL CUTTING TO COMPLETE THE QUILT

From the tan print, cut:
3 strips, 9½" × 42"; crosscut into 9 squares, 9½" × 9½"

From the red print, cut:
2 strips, 14" × 42"; crosscut into:
- 3 squares, 14" × 14"; cut the squares into quarters diagonally to yield 12 side triangles
- 2 squares, 7¼" × 7¼"; cut the squares in half diagonally to yield 4 corner triangles

4 strips, 3½" × 42"; crosscut into 36 squares, 3½" × 3½"

From the beige print, cut:
6 strips, 2" × 42"

From the brown print, cut:
7 strips, 2" × 42"

From the brown print, cut on the *lengthwise* grain:
2 strips, 6½" × 66½"
2 strips, 6½" × 54½"

Pieced by Mary Ellen Robison and Paula Barnes;
quilted by Marcella Pickett

Weathervane

MAKING THE WEATHERVANE BLOCK

The instructions below are for making one block at a time. Repeat to piece eight pairs of blocks (16 total). Press seam allowances in the directions indicated by the arrows.

1 Select a set of pieces cut for one block. Referring to "Half-Square-Triangle Units" on page 77, mark the light 2½" squares and layer them right sides together with the dark A 2½" squares. Sew, cut, press, and trim to 2" square. Make eight half-square-triangle units.

Make 8 units.

2 Lay out one light 2" square, two half-square-triangle units, and one dark B square in two rows of two. The light and dark prints should be the same throughout. Sew the squares and pieced units into rows. Join the rows to make a four-patch unit measuring 3½" square, including seam allowances. Make four units.

Make 4 units, 3½" × 3½".

3 Draw a diagonal line from corner to corner on the wrong side of the remaining light 2" squares. Place a marked square on one corner of a dark C square, right sides together. Sew on the marked line. Trim the excess corner fabric, ¼" from the stitched line. Place a marked square on an adjacent corner of the dark C square. Sew and trim as before to make a side unit measuring 3½" square, including seam allowances. Make four units.

Make 4 units, 3½" × 3½".

4 Lay out four four-patch units, four side units, and one dark D square in three rows, rotating the units as shown. Sew the units and square into rows. Join the rows to make a Weathervane block measuring 9½" square, including seam allowances.

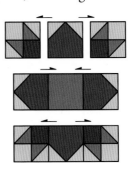 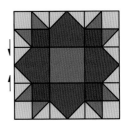

Make 1 Weathervane block, 9½" × 9½".

5 Repeat steps 1–4 to make a total of 16 blocks.

Quilt Club

MAKING THE SNOWBALL BLOCKS

Draw a diagonal line from corner to corner on the wrong side of the red 3½" squares. Place a marked square on each corner of a tan square. Sew on the marked lines. Trim the excess corner fabric ¼" from the stitched line. Make nine Snowball blocks measuring 9½" square, including seam allowances.

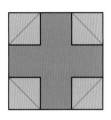
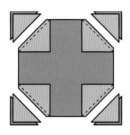

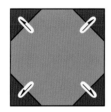

Make 9 Snowball blocks,
9½" × 9½".

ASSEMBLING THE QUILT TOP

1 Referring to the quilt assembly diagram below, arrange and sew the Weathervane and Snowball blocks together in diagonal rows, adding the side triangles to the ends of each row as indicated. Join the rows, adding the corner triangles last.

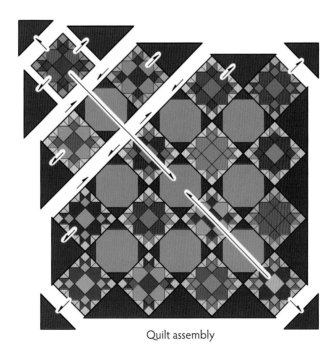

Quilt assembly

Weathervane

3 Join the beige strips end to end. From the pieced strip, cut two 54½"-long strips and two 51½"-long strips. Sew the shorter strips to opposite sides of the quilt center. Sew the longer strips to the top and bottom edges. Press the seam allowances toward the beige strips. The quilt top should measure 54½" square, including seam allowances.

4 Sew the brown 54½"-long strips to opposite sides of the quilt top. Sew the brown 66½"-long strips to the top and bottom edges to complete the quilt top. Press the seam allowances toward the brown strips. The quilt top should measure 66½" square.

FINISHING THE QUILT

For more details on any finishing steps, visit ShopMartingale.com/HowtoQuilt for free downloadable information.

1 Layer the quilt top with batting and backing; baste the layers together.

2 Quilt by hand or machine. The quilt shown is machine quilted with feather wreaths in the Snowball blocks and a half wreath in the setting triangles. A feather motif is stitched in the Weathervane blocks. Curved lines and plumes are stitched in the outer border.

3 Make double-fold binding using the brown 2"-wide strips. Attach the binding to the quilt.

2 Trim and square up the quilt top, making sure to leave ¼" beyond the points of all blocks for seam allowances. The quilt top should measure 51½" square, including seam allowances.

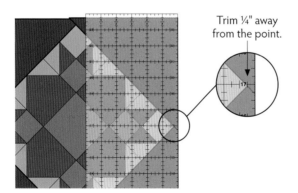

Trim ¼" away from the point.

Little Sawtooth

Believe it or not, Little Sawtooth uses the same size and almost the same number of half-square-triangle units as Mosaic on page 43. Yet these quilts couldn't look more different! In Mosaic, the little triangles are stitched into blocks. Here, they work to frame much larger half-square-triangle units. When trading units with friends, it will be fun to see which layout everyone chooses for their quilts.

Exchanging the Half-Square-Triangle Units

This exchange is for 10 participants. Each participant will make 10 sets of 80 half-square-triangle units each (800 total). After making the units, place eight half-square-triangle units from each set in a resealable bag so that you have 10 bags with 80 different units in each bag. After the exchange, each participant will have an assortment of 800 half-square-triangle units. Use them to make Little Sawtooth blocks and assemble the quilt as instructed on page 58 or create your own unique blocks and quilt layout.

Finished quilt: 82½" × 92½"

Finished block: 10" × 10"

MATERIALS

Yardage is based on 42"-wide fabric.

½ yard *each* of 10 assorted light prints for half-square-triangle units*

½ yard *each* of 10 assorted dark prints for half-square-triangle units*

2⅝ yards of cream print for blocks

2⅝ yards of navy A print for blocks

¾ yard of navy B print for binding

7⅝ yards of fabric for backing

91" × 101" piece of batting

2" finished Star Singles papers (optional)**

*If you're using scraps, you'll need 100 dark and 100 light 7" squares.

**See "Using Star Singles" on page 57 before cutting fabrics.

Using Star Singles

If you use the 2" Star Singles papers, do not cut the 3" squares from the light and dark prints. Instead, skip "Making the Half-Square-Triangle Units" at right and follow the directions on the package to cut the following pieces.

From *each* of the assorted light prints, cut:

2 strips, 6½" × 42"; crosscut into 10 squares, 6½" × 6½" (100 total)

From *each* of the assorted dark prints, cut:

2 strips, 6½" × 42"; crosscut into 10 squares, 6½" × 6½" (100 total)

CUTTING

All measurements include ¼" seam allowances. Our instructions for traditional half-square-triangle units are for cutting pieces slightly oversized so you can trim them accurately when done.

CUTTING FOR HALF-SQUARE-TRIANGLE UNITS

From *each* of the assorted light prints, cut:

4 strips, 3" × 42"; crosscut into 40 squares, 3" × 3" (400 total)

From *each* of the assorted dark prints, cut:

4 strips, 3" × 42"; crosscut into 40 squares, 3" × 3" (400 total)

ADDITIONAL CUTTING TO COMPLETE THE QUILT

From the cream print, cut:

9 strips, 9¼" × 42"; crosscut into 36 squares, 9¼" × 9¼"

From navy A print, cut:

9 strips, 9¼" × 42"; crosscut into 36 squares, 9¼" × 9¼"

From navy B print, cut:

9 strips, 2" × 42"

MAKING THE HALF-SQUARE-TRIANGLE UNITS

Press seam allowances in the directions indicated by the arrows. Referring to "Half-Square-Triangle Units" on page 77, mark the light 3" squares and layer them right sides together with the dark 3" squares. Sew, cut, press, and trim to 2½" square. Make 10 sets of 80 matching half-square-triangle units (800 total).

Make 800 units total.

MAKING THE LITTLE SAWTOOTH BLOCKS

1 Lay out four half-square-triangle units, orienting them as shown. Join the units to make a bottom unit measuring 2½" × 8½", including seam allowances. Make 72 units. In the same way, make 72 side units as shown, being sure to reverse the position of the dark triangles. The side units should measure 2½" × 8½", including seam allowances.

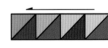

Make 72 bottom units, 2½" × 8½".

Make 72 side units, 2½" × 8½".

3 Lay out one triangle unit from step 2, one bottom unit and one side unit from step 1, and one small half-square-triangle unit as shown. Sew the units into rows. Join the rows to make a Little Sawtooth block measuring 10½" square, including seam allowances. Make 72 blocks.

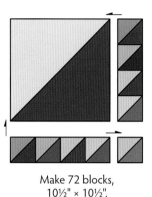

Make 72 blocks,
10½" × 10½".

ASSEMBLING THE QUILT TOP

Instead of making a long side border, we find it easier to sew the side border units to the end of each block row. Adding the border units in this way helps to eliminate a wavy border.

1 Lay out five small half-square-triangle units, orienting them as shown. Join the units to make a top border unit measuring 2½" × 10½", including seam allowances. Make eight units.

 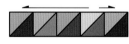

Make 8 top border units,
2½" × 10½".

2 Lay out five small half-square-triangle units, orienting them as shown. Join the units to make a side border unit measuring 2½" × 10½", including seam allowances. Make nine units.

Make 9 side border units,
2½" × 10½".

2 Mark the cream squares and layer them right sides together with the navy A squares. Sew, cut, press, and trim to 8½" square. Make 72 large half-square-triangle units.

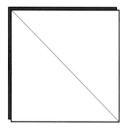 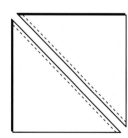

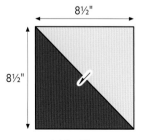

8½"

8½"

Make 72 units.

Quilt Club

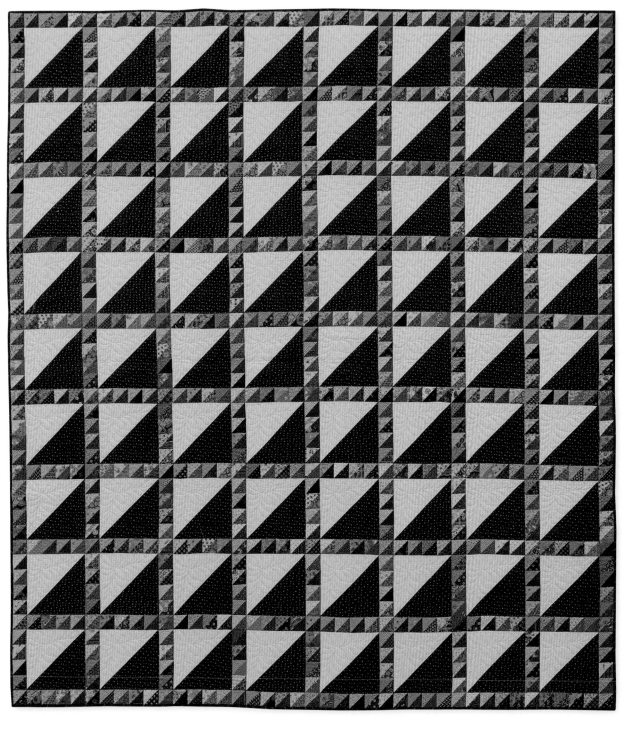

Pieced by Mary Ellen Robison; quilted by Sarabeth Rebe

Little Sawtooth

3 Lay out the blocks in nine rows of eight blocks each as shown in the quilt assembly diagram below. Add the top and side border units plus one half-square-triangle unit in the upper-left corner, making sure to orient the units as shown. Sew the blocks and units into rows. Join the rows to complete the quilt top. The quilt top should measure 82½" × 92½". You'll have 66 triangle units left over for another project.

FINISHING THE QUILT

For more details on any finishing steps, visit ShopMartingale.com/HowtoQuilt for free downloadable information.

1 Layer the quilt top with batting and backing; baste the layers together.

2 Quilt by hand or machine. The quilt shown is machine quilted with a feather motif in each of the large triangles. A continuous swirl motif is stitched in the small triangles.

3 Make double-fold binding using the navy B 2"-wide strips. Attach the binding to the quilt.

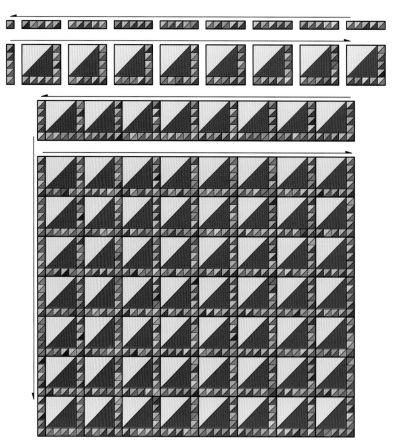

Quilt assembly

Tree

The Tree block is one of our favorites and there are many delightful variations of it. For this exchange, we opted for a variety of background fabrics that are busier than many quilters are used to. We chose those instead of shirtings and very light prints. As a counterpoint, we concentrated on small-scale prints for the darks. The result is quite dramatic!

Exchanging the Blocks

This exchange is for 12 participants. Each participant will make three sets of 12 blocks (36 total). After the blocks are made, place one block from each set in a resealable bag so that you have 12 bags with three different blocks in each bag. After the exchange, each participant will have 36 different Tree blocks. Use them to assemble the quilt as instructed on page 66 or create your own unique quilt layout.

Finished quilt: 90¾" × 90¾"
Finished block: 9" × 9"

MATERIALS

Yardage is based on 42"-wide fabric.

1⅓ yards *each* of 3 assorted light prints for blocks*

1 yard *each* of 3 assorted dark prints for blocks*

6⅞ yards of navy print for setting squares, setting triangles, outer border, and binding

½ yard of tan print for inner border

8¼ yards of fabric for backing

99" × 99" piece of batting

1½" finished Star Singles papers (optional)**

*Yardage is for making blocks for swapping. If you are making this quilt on your own, you will need 4⅛ yards total of assorted light scraps and 3⅛ yards total of assorted dark scraps.

**See "Using Star Singles" on page 63 before cutting fabrics.

Using Star Singles

If you use the 1½" Star Singles papers, do not cut the 2½" squares from the light and dark prints. Instead, skip step 1 of "Making the Tree Blocks" below right and follow the directions on the package to cut the following pieces.

From *each* of the assorted light prints, cut:

4 strips, 5½" × 42"; crosscut into 24 squares, 5½" × 5½" (72 total)

From *each* of the assorted dark prints, cut:

4 strips, 5½" × 42"; crosscut into 24 squares, 5½" × 5½" (72 total)

CUTTING

You'll need 36 blocks to complete the featured quilt. Cutting is given for one block at a time; the number of pieces listed in parentheses provides the total amount needed to make 36 blocks. (See "Exchanging the Blocks" on page 61.) For greater ease in piecing the blocks, keep the pieces for each block grouped together. All measurements include ¼" seam allowances.

CUTTING FOR 1 BLOCK

From *1* light print, cut:

1 square, 5" × 5" (18 total)

2 pieces, 2¾" × 4¼" (72 total)

8 squares, 2½" × 2½" (288 total)

4 squares, 2" × 2" (144 total)

From *1* dark print, cut:

1 square, 5" × 5" (18 total)

1 square, 2¾" × 2¾" (36 total)

8 squares, 2½" × 2½" (288 total)

4 squares, 1⅝" × 1⅝" (144 total)

ADDITIONAL CUTTING TO COMPLETE THE QUILT

From the navy print, cut:

3 strips, 14" × 42"; crosscut into:

- 5 squares, 14" × 14"; cut the squares into quarters diagonally to yield 20 side triangles
- 2 squares, 7¼" × 7¼"; cut the squares in half diagonally to yield 4 corner triangles

7 strips, 9½" × 42"; crosscut into 25 squares, 9½" × 9½"

10 strips, 2" × 42"

From the tan print, cut:

8 strips, 1½" × 42"

From the remainder of the navy print, cut on the *lengthwise* grain:

2 strips, 6½" × 90¾"

2 strips, 6½" × 78¾"

MAKING THE TREE BLOCKS

The instructions below are for making one block. Each block uses the pieces cut from one light print and one dark print. Repeat to piece three sets of 12 blocks (36 total). Press seam allowances in the directions indicated by the arrows.

1 Select a set of pieces cut for one block. Referring to "Half-Square-Triangle Units" on page 77, mark the light 2½" squares and layer them right sides together with the dark 2½" squares. Sew, cut, press, and trim to 2" square. Make 16 small half-square-triangle units.

Make 16 units.

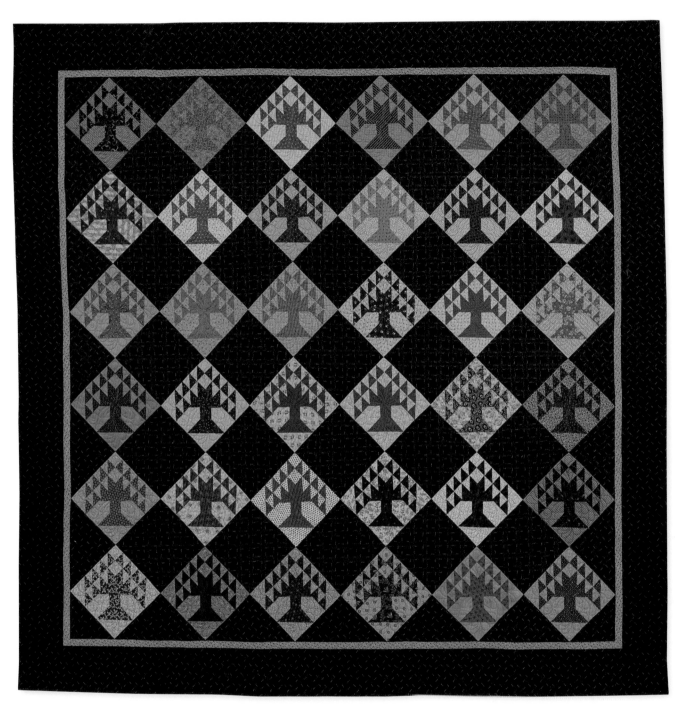

Pieced by Mary Ellen Robison; quilted by Sarabeth Rebe

2 Mark the light 5" square and layer it right sides together with the dark 5" square. Sew, cut, press, and trim each unit to 4¼" square. Make two large half-square-triangle units. Set aside one unit for another block.

 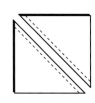 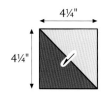

Make 2 units.

3 Lay out two light 2" squares and two small half-square-triangle units in two rows of two. Sew the squares and units into rows. Join the rows to make a corner unit measuring 3½" square, including seam allowances.

Make 1 unit,
3½" × 3½".

4 Lay out one light 2" square and seven small half-square-triangle units in two rows, noting the orientation of the units. Sew the square and units into rows. Join the rows to make a side unit measuring 3½" × 6½", including seam allowances.

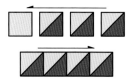 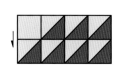

Make 1 side unit,
3½" × 6½".

5 Repeat step 4, rotating the units according to the diagram to make one reversed side unit.

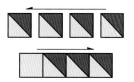 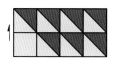

Make 1 reversed side unit,
3½" × 6½".

6 Draw a diagonal line from corner to corner on the wrong side of the dark 1⅝" squares. Place a marked square on one corner of a light 2¾" × 4¼" piece, right sides together. Sew on the marked line. Trim the excess corner fabric ¼" from the stitched line. Place a matching square on an adjacent corner of the light piece. Sew and trim as before to make a treetop unit measuring 2¾" × 4¼", including seam allowances. Make two units.

Make 2 units,
2¾" × 4¼".

Tree

7 Lay out two treetop units from step 6, one large half-square-triangle unit from step 2, and one dark 2¾" square in two rows, noting the orientation of the units. Sew the square and units into rows. Join the rows to make a tree-trunk unit measuring 6½" square, including seam allowances.

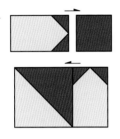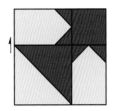

Make 1 unit,
6½" × 6½".

Something Special

It's always nice to include a little gift with your exchange blocks—nothing expensive, just maybe a pack of notes or a little paintbrush to clean out the sewing machine after a long day of stitching. And there's always chocolate!

8 Lay out a side unit, a corner unit, a tree-trunk unit, and a reversed side unit in two rows. The light and dark prints should be the same in all of the units. Sew the units into rows. Join the rows to make a Tree block measuring 9½" square, including seam allowances.

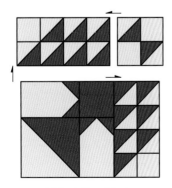

Make 1 Tree block,
9½" × 9½".

9 Repeat steps 1–8 to make a total of 36 blocks.

ASSEMBLING THE QUILT TOP

1 Referring to the quilt assembly diagram, arrange and sew the blocks and navy squares together in diagonal rows, adding the side triangles to the ends of each row as indicated. Join the rows, adding the corner triangles last.

Quilt assembly

2 Trim and square up the quilt top, making sure to leave ¼" beyond the points of all blocks for seam allowances. The quilt top should measure 76¾" square, including seam allowances.

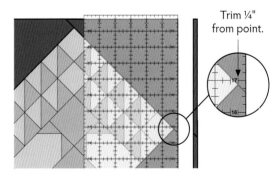

Trim ¼"
from point.

3 Join the tan 1½"-wide strips end to end. From the pieced strip, cut two 78¾"-long strips and two 76¾"-long strips. Sew the shorter strips to opposite sides of the quilt top. Sew the longer strips to the top and bottom edges. Press the seam allowances toward the tan strips. The quilt top should measure 78¾" square, including seam allowances.

4 Sew the navy 78¾"-long strips to opposite sides of the quilt top. Sew the navy 90¾"-long strips to the top and bottom edges to complete the quilt top. Press the seam allowances toward the navy strips. The quilt top should measure 90¾" square.

FINISHING THE QUILT

For more details on any finishing steps, visit ShopMartingale.com/HowtoQuilt for free downloadable information.

1 Layer the quilt top with batting and backing; baste the layers together.

2 Quilt by hand or machine. The quilt shown is machine quilted with a feather motif in the blocks and setting squares. A continuous feather motif is stitched in the outer border.

3 Make double-fold binding using the navy 2"-wide strips. Attach the binding to the quilt.

Fancy

A classic blue-and-white quilt never goes out of style. We chose different shades of blues combined with soft cream shirtings to complete this beautiful wall quilt. The key to this exchange is to make sure the navy you choose for your blocks is darker than all the other blues, since the navy fabric forms the central Nine Patch and the chain throughout the blocks.

Exchanging the Blocks

This exchange is for nine participants.
Each participant will make nine identical blocks. After the blocks are made, place each block in a resealable bag so that you have nine bags. After the exchange, each participant will have nine different Fancy blocks. Use them to assemble the quilt as instructed on page 75 or create your own unique quilt layout.

Finished quilt: 72½" × 72½"
Finished block: 13" × 13"

MATERIALS

Yardage is based on 42"-wide fabric.

1 yard of light A print for blocks*

⅞ yard of light B print for blocks*

½ yard of navy A print for blocks

⅛ yard of blue A print for blocks*

¾ yard of blue B print for blocks*

½ yard of blue C print for blocks*

1⅞ yards of cream print for setting squares, setting triangles, and middle border

3⅛ yards of navy B print for inner and outer borders and binding

4½ yards of fabric for backing

79" × 79" piece of batting

2" finished Star Singles papers (optional)**

*Yardage is for making blocks for swapping. If you are making this quilt on your own, you will need 1⅞ yards total of assorted light prints and 1⅜ yards total of assorted blue prints.

**See "Using Star Singles" on page 70 before cutting fabrics.

Using Star Singles

If you use the 2" Star Singles papers, *do not* cut the 3" squares from the light A and blue B prints. Instead, skip step 1 of "Making the Fancy Blocks" on page 73 and follow the directions on the package to cut the following pieces.

From the light A print, cut:

2 strips, 6½" × 42"; crosscut into 9 squares, 6½" × 6½"

From the blue B print, cut:

2 strips, 6½" × 42"; crosscut into 9 squares, 6½" × 6½"

CUTTING

All measurements include ¼" seam allowances.

CUTTING FOR BLOCKS

From the light A print, cut:

3 strips, 3" × 42"; crosscut into 36 squares, 3" × 3"

6 strips, 2½" × 42"; crosscut into 36 pieces, 2½" × 5½"

3 strips, 1½" × 42"

From the light B print, cut:

3 strips, 4½" × 42"; crosscut into 18 squares, 4½" × 4½". Cut the squares into quarters diagonally to yield 72 triangles.

3 strips, 2½" × 42"

4 strips, 1½" × 42"

From the navy A print, cut:

11 strips, 1½" × 42"; crosscut *1 of the strips* into 2 strips, 1½" × 21" (1 is extra)

From the blue A print, cut:

2 strips, 1½" × 42"; crosscut *1 of the strips* into 2 strips, 1½" × 21"

From the blue B print, cut:

3 strips, 3" × 42"; crosscut into 36 squares, 3" × 3"

5 strips, 2½" × 42"; crosscut into 72 squares, 2½" × 2½"

From the blue C print, cut:

3 strips, 4½" × 42"; crosscut into 18 squares, 4½" × 4½". Cut the squares into quarters diagonally to yield 72 triangles.

ADDITIONAL CUTTING TO COMPLETE THE QUILT

From the cream print, cut:

1 strip, 19¾" × 42"; crosscut into 2 squares, 19¾" × 19¾". Cut the squares into quarters diagonally to yield 8 side triangles.

2 strips, 13½" × 42"; crosscut into:

- 4 squares, 13½" × 13½"
- 2 squares, 10⅛" × 10⅛"; cut the squares in half diagonally to yield 4 corner triangles

6 strips, 1½" × 42"

From the navy B print, cut:

8 strips, 2" × 42"

6 strips, 1½" × 42"

From the remainder of the navy B print, cut on the *lengthwise* grain:

2 strips, 7" × 72½"

2 strips, 7" × 59½"

MAKING THE UNITS

Press seam allowances in the directions indicated by the arrows.

1 Sew light A and navy A 1½" × 42" strips together in pairs to make three strip sets measuring 2½" × 42", including seam allowances. Cut the strip sets into 72 segments, 1½" × 2½".

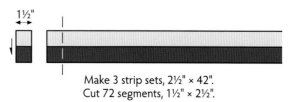

Make 3 strip sets, 2½" × 42".
Cut 72 segments, 1½" × 2½".

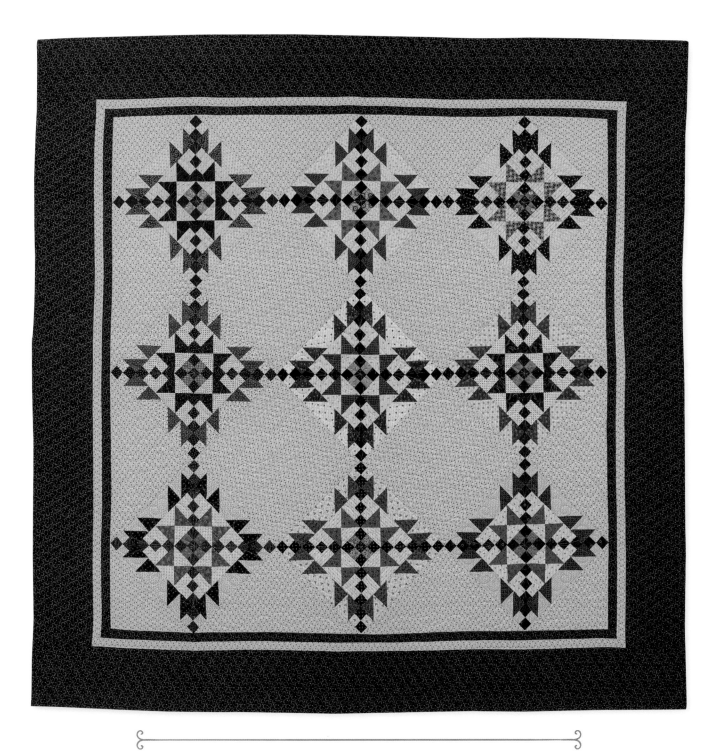

Pieced by Mary Ellen Robison; quilted by Sarabeth Rebe

2 Join two segments from step 1 to make a four-patch unit. Make 36 units measuring 2½" square, including seam allowances.

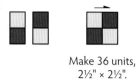

Make 36 units,
2½" × 2½".

3 Sew together navy A 1½"-wide and light B 2½"-wide strips to make three strip sets measuring 3½" × 42", including seam allowances. Cut the strip sets into 72 segments, 1½" × 3½".

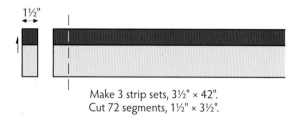

Make 3 strip sets, 3½" × 42".
Cut 72 segments, 1½" × 3½".

4 Sew a light B 1½"-wide strip to each long side of a navy A 1½" × 42" strip to make a strip set measuring 3½" × 42", including seam allowances. Make two strip sets. Cut the strip sets into 36 segments, 1½" × 3½".

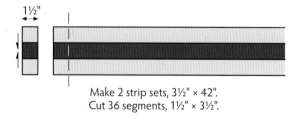

Make 2 strip sets, 3½" × 42".
Cut 36 segments, 1½" × 3½".

5 Join two segments from step 3 and one segment from step 4 to make a corner unit. Make 36 units measuring 3½" square, including seam allowances.

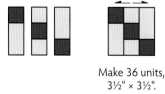

Make 36 units,
3½" × 3½".

6 Sew a navy A 1½" × 42" strip to each long side of a blue A 1½" × 42" strip to make a strip set measuring 3½" × 42", including seam allowances. Cut the strip set into 18 segments, 1½" × 3½".

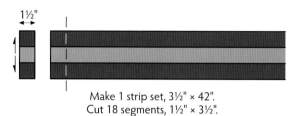

Make 1 strip set, 3½" × 42".
Cut 18 segments, 1½" × 3½".

7 Sew a blue A 1½" × 21" strip to each long side of a navy A 1½" × 21" strip to make a strip set measuring 3½" × 21", including seam allowances. Cut the strip set into nine segments, 1½" × 3½".

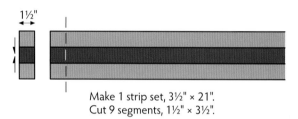

Make 1 strip set, 3½" × 21".
Cut 9 segments, 1½" × 3½".

8 Join two segments from step 6 and one segment from step 7 to make a nine-patch unit. Make nine units measuring 3½" square, including seam allowances.

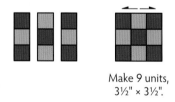

Make 9 units,
3½" × 3½".

MAKING THE FANCY BLOCKS

1 Referring to "Half-Square-Triangle Units" on page 77, mark the light A 3" squares and layer them right sides together with the blue B 3" squares. Sew, cut, press, and trim the units to 2½" square. Make 72 half-square-triangle units.

Make 72 units.

2 Draw a diagonal line from corner to corner on the wrong side of the blue B 2½" squares. Place marked squares on each end of a light A 2½" × 5½" piece, right sides together. Sew on the marked lines. Trim the excess corner fabric ¼" from the stitched lines. Make 36 units measuring 2½" × 5½", including seam allowances.

Make 36 units,
2½" × 5½".

3 Join two half-square-triangle units and one unit from step 2 to make a side unit. Make 36 units measuring 2½" × 9½", including seam allowances.

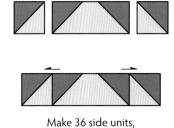

Make 36 side units,
2½" × 9½".

4 Sew a light B and blue C triangle together as shown. Make 72 pieced triangle units. Join two units to make an hourglass unit. Make 36 units.

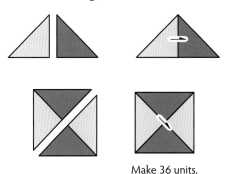

Make 36 units.

5 Align the 45° line of a square ruler with the diagonal seamline on an hourglass unit as shown, making sure that the 1¾" lines on the ruler meet in the center of the block, and the 3½" lines meet on the diagonal seamlines. Trim along the top and right edges of the ruler.

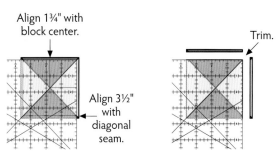

Align 1¾" with block center.

Align 3½" with diagonal seam.

Trim.

lines. The hourglass units should form a star. Sew the units into rows. Join the rows to make a center unit. Make nine units measuring 9½" square, including seam allowances.

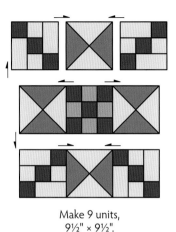

Make 9 units,
9½" × 9½".

8 Lay out four of the four-patch units, four side units, and one center unit in three rows, rotating the four-patch units so that the navy squares are in the outer corners. The side units should form a star. Sew the units into rows. Join the rows to make a Fancy block. Make nine blocks measuring 13½" square, including seam allowances.

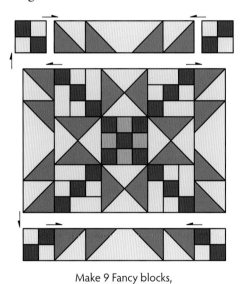

Make 9 Fancy blocks,
13½" × 13½".

6 Rotate the block 180° so that you can trim the other sides. Align the 45° line of the ruler with the diagonal seamline of the block, making sure the 1¾" lines meet in the center. The 3½" lines on the ruler should align with the previously cut edges. Trim along the top and right sides of the square ruler. Repeat the trimming steps for each hourglass unit. The units should measure 3½" square, including seam allowances.

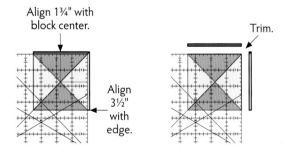

Align 1¾" with block center.

Trim.

Align 3½" with edge.

7 Lay out four corner units, four hourglass units, and one nine-patch unit in three rows, rotating the corner units so that the navy squares form diagonal

Quilt Club

ASSEMBLING THE QUILT TOP

1 Referring to the quilt assembly diagram, arrange and sew the blocks and cream squares together in diagonal rows, adding the side triangles to the ends of each row as indicated. Join the rows, adding the corner triangles last.

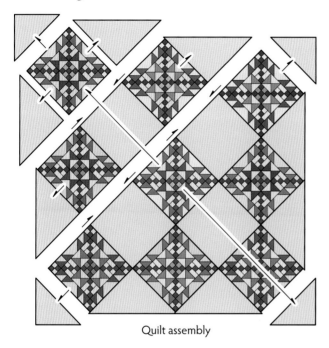

Quilt assembly

2 Trim and square up the quilt top, making sure to leave ¼" beyond the points of all blocks for seam allowances. The quilt top should measure 55½" square, including seam allowances.

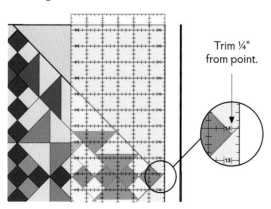

Trim ¼" from point.

3 Sew the navy B 1½"-wide strips together end to end. From the pieced strip, cut two 57½"-long strips and two 55½"-long strips. Sew the shorter strips to opposite sides of the quilt center. Sew the longer strips to the top and bottom edges. Press the seam allowances toward the navy strips. The quilt top should measure 57½" square, including seam allowances.

4 Sew the cream 1½"-wide strips together end to end. From the pieced strip, cut two 59½"-long strips and two 57½"-long strips. Sew the shorter strips to opposite sides of the quilt top. Sew the longer strips to the top and bottom edges. Press the seam allowances toward the cream strips. The quilt top should measure 59½" square, including seam allowances.

5 Sew the navy B 59½"-long strips to opposite sides of the quilt top. Sew the navy B 72½"-long strips to the top and bottom edges to complete the quilt top. Press the seam allowances toward the navy strips. The quilt top should measure 72½" square.

FINISHING THE QUILT

For more details on any finishing steps, visit ShopMartingale.com/HowtoQuilt for free downloadable information.

1 Layer the quilt top with batting and backing; baste the layers together.

2 Quilt by hand or machine. The quilt shown is machine quilted with a feather motif in the setting squares and triangles. A plume design is stitched in the blocks. A continuous feather motif is stitched in the outer border.

3 Make double-fold binding using the navy B 2"-wide strips. Attach the binding to the quilt.

Quiltmaking Basics

Quiltmaking is the result of fabrics, tools, and skills coming together in a wonderful combination. With the right fabrics, the proper tools, and basic sewing skills, anyone can make a quilt. The questions then become: "What are the right fabrics? What are the proper tools? And what skills are needed?" We hope to answer those questions here in addition to providing specific instructions for constructing half-square-triangle units.

FABRIC

How to choose the right fabrics? If you're like most quilters, you probably have more than enough fabric already, and most of it could even be considered "right." But do feel free to shop! (You know you want to!) Most of the quilts featured in this book were designed and pieced using 1800s reproduction fabrics. Fabrics reminiscent of that time period include plaids, checks, stripes, polka dots, and shirtings, in color palettes that encompass blues, blacks, browns, madder reds and turkey reds, cheddars, bubblegum pinks, and poison greens. These are the prints and colors that we love and prefer to work with, but that shouldn't prevent you from piecing any of these quilts in fabrics that you consider to be right—perhaps batiks or even a combination of fabric styles. These will be your quilts; experiment with favorite fabrics.

TOOLS

The proper tools of the quiltmaking trade include rotary cutters, rulers, cutting mats, sharp scissors, all-cotton thread, and your favorite sewing machine in good working order (clean, oiled, and ready to go).

Rotary cutter and cutting mat. Always keep a sharp blade in your rotary cutter. It will help with accuracy and ensure that your fabric is cut smoothly. The cutting mat should be as large as your space allows.

Rulers. Our favorite ruler size for cutting strips and borders is the 6½" × 24" ruler, but square rulers are very handy for squaring up blocks. The 6½" and 9½" square rulers are the sizes we use most often.

Thread. We prefer 100% cotton thread to blend with the cotton fabrics in our quilts.

SKILLS

We all come to quiltmaking with varying skill levels and experiences, but accuracy is the most important qualification needed to successfully complete a quilt. Let's start with accuracy in cutting.

The instructions for all the projects in this book involve rotary cutting, and a standard ¼"-wide seam allowance is included in all measurements. Before you begin cutting, we suggest starching and pressing your fabric well. Put a new blade in your rotary cutter. These are basic steps that go a long way toward successful cutting.

An accurate ¼" seam allowance is also essential in quiltmaking. Consider purchasing a ¼" presser foot for your sewing machine. Whether you use a ¼" foot or a standard foot, take the time to test your accuracy before you begin piecing your project. To check accuracy, follow these steps.

1 Cut three 1½" × 4" strips.

2 Sew the strips together. Press the seam allowances toward the outer strips.

3 Using a ruler, measure the width of the center strip. It should measure 1". If your center strip is larger than 1", your seam allowance is too narrow. If your center strip is smaller than 1", your seam allowance is too wide. Cut new strips and repeat until the center strip measures exactly 1".

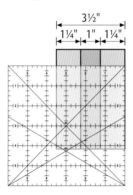

You can also use ¼" graph paper to check your seam allowance. Place a piece of the graph paper under the presser foot and sew on the first ¼" line. Affix a piece of painter's tape or ¼" quilter's tape along the edge of the paper. Remove the graph paper and sew three strips together using the seam guide, and then check the center strip for accuracy. Once you know the seam guide is in the correct position, build it up with another layer or two of tape.

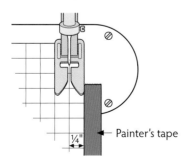

Painter's tape

After sewing seams accurately, pressing becomes the next important step. Recommended pressing directions for seam allowances are included throughout the project instructions. Remember, you are pressing to set seams, not ironing the wrinkles out of a shirt.

HALF-SQUARE-TRIANGLE UNITS

We love half-square-triangle units, as you can see from our quilts! They add so much to a simple block. There are many different methods and tools available for making them, and you may already have a favorite technique. If so, feel free to use it. For these projects, we've generally used the technique of piecing the units from layered squares, without cutting triangles first.

We've also provided cutting options for the projects in which purchased triangle papers would be a good option. We like the ease and accuracy of Star Singles papers, designed by Liz Eagan of Spinning Star Design, and we often use them in our quiltmaking. They make several identical half-square-triangle units at a time. Star Singles are widely available at quilt shops and online.

When making half-square-triangle units without the papers, we cut squares oversized and trim the final units after pressing. This guarantees complete accuracy.

In the steps that follow, we've used 1" finished half-square-triangle units as an example.

1 Cut a light and a dark square, 1¼" larger than the desired finished size. In this case, cut the squares 2¼" × 2¼".

2 With a pencil or fabric marker and ruler, draw a diagonal line from corner to corner on the wrong side of the lighter 2¼" square.

3 Place the marked square on the dark 2¼" square with right sides together. Align the raw edges and sew ¼" from both sides of the marked line.

Mark diagonal.   Sew ¼" from each
                   side of the line.

4 Cut on the marked line. You'll have two identical half-square-triangle units. Press seam allowances toward the darker triangle.

Cut on marked line.   Press.

5 Using a square ruler, trim the units to 1½" square, aligning the 45° line of your ruler with the seam. Make sure that the unit under the ruler extends beyond the 1½" marks, and trim the right and top edges with your rotary cutter. Rotate the unit 180°, align the newly cut edges with the 1½" marks, and trim the right and top edges.

Align 1½" with
diagonal seam.
                                        Trim.

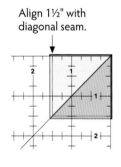 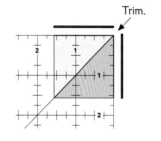

Align 1½"
with edge.
                                        Trim.

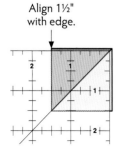 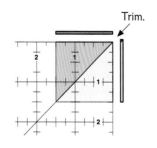

QUILTING

Your top is complete, so now it's time to prepare it for quilting. For many of us, that means making a backing and passing the project on to a machine quilter. The pattern instructions provide our yardage recommendations for a pieced backing. They allow for at least 3" to 4" extra on each side of the quilt, or a backing that's 6" to 8" larger than the finished quilt dimensions.

BINDING

We most often use a double-fold, straight-grain binding on our quilts, but we cut our strips 2" wide, which is slightly narrower than what is often suggested. We find this width provides a nice, tight binding. Each project indicates the number of binding strips to cut, and the yardage is enough that you can cut 2½"-wide strips if you prefer, either across the fabric width or on the bias.

We have learned that binding cut on the lengthwise grain is not recommended. Crossgrain strips have more flexibility and stretch, ensuring that your quilt will lie flat when bound. Sew the strips end to end to make the continuous binding you will need.

Don't Forget a Label

Now that your quilt is finished, please remember to add a label. Some things to include, in addition to your full name, are the date you began the quilt, the date you completed it, your hometown, the name of the quilter (if not you), and the name of the recipient (if the quilt is a gift).

Acknowledgments

As we finished this, our third book, we took a moment to look back and remember all the people who helped us get here. While our names are on the cover, we certainly didn't do this alone. Paula handles the design and pattern writing, and Mary Ellen takes care of piecing the tops and writing the text. After those tasks are completed, we look to others for much-needed help. Now we would like to acknowledge and thank each of those generous people.

First, a very special thank-you to the wonderful team at Martingale. You have believed in us and supported us throughout the entire process. Because of your dedication and attention to detail, we ended up with a beautiful finished project.

Our quilters are next on the list, and without them we would have a lot of quilt tops. It's their quilting talent and skill that takes our quilts to the next level. Our gratitude goes to Marcella Pickett and Margie Love of Crooked Creek Quilts, Sarabeth Rebe of Cotton Luv Quilts, Sharon Dixon of Katy T-Shirt Quilts, Cathy Peters and Lynn Graham, and Pat Meeks.

Let's not forget our loyal customers and fans. We don't know where we would be without your continued support. Thank you for always making us feel special.

We would like to thank Pam Buda of Heartspun Quilts and author of *Vintage Patchwork* (Martingale, 2018) and *Vintage Treasures* (Martingale, 2020) for sharing her exchange guides with us and for allowing us to use them in this book.

And of course, last but not least, a special thank-you to our families. You have been there for all of Red Crinoline Quilts' adventures. Guess you know what you're getting for Christmas. Make room on the bookshelf for another one of Mom's books.

Paula Barnes (right) and Mary Ellen Robison (left) met more than 20 years ago when they both moved to the same street in Katy, Texas. Paula taught quilting classes at the local quilt shop, and Mary Ellen was the devoted student. They quickly formed a friendship that went beyond their love of quilting and reproduction fabric to become Red Crinoline Quilts. Although they met in Texas, each one comes from a different part of the country. Mary Ellen was born and raised in New York, while Paula is from Georgia. Theirs is a true North-South friendship.

Mary Ellen and her husband, Peter, live in St. Petersburg, Florida, where she divides her time between sewing quilts for Red Crinoline Quilts, cruising, and traveling to see her three children and their families—Megan, son-in-law Brian, and grandson Adam in Louisville, Kentucky; Brett, daughter-in-law Meredith, and granddaughters Sydney and Julianne in Ballston Lake, New York; and Caitlin in Tampa, Florida.

Paula lives in the Dallas area and is mom to three grown daughters, Alison, Ashley, and Amy; mother-in-law to three sons-in-law, David, Robert, and Alex; and grandmother (or MiMi) to granddaughter Sophie and grandsons John and Walker. Paula began teaching quilting in 1989 in Dallas, and now travels throughout the United States, teaching and lecturing at quilt guilds and local quilt shops.

You can contact both Mary Ellen and Paula at Red Crinoline Quilts
(info@redcrinolinequilts.com).